Dear Sister, Dear Sister!
A Collection of Sisterhood Letters
From Trade Union Women

edited by Nancy Riche

Canadian Centre for Policy Alternatives
2002

National Library of Canada Cataloguing in Publication Data

Dear Sister, Dear Sister! : a collection of sisterhood letters from trade union women / Nancy Riche, editor.

ISBN 0-88627-296-3

1. Women labor union members—Canada. I. Riche, Nancy II. Canadian Centre for Policy Alternatives

HD6079.2.C3D42 2002   331.4'78'0971   C2002-902486-2

Printed and bound in Canada

Published by

Canadian Centre for Policy Alternatives
Suite 410, 75 Albert Street
Ottawa, ON K1P 5E7
Tel 613-563-1341   Fax 613-233-1458
http://www.policyalternatives.ca
ccpa@policyalternatives.ca

Contents

Contributors

Phyllis Benedict
President, Elementary Teachers' Federation of Ontario

Ruth Bergman,
Kenora & District Labour Council, Past President
NUPGE/OPSEU Local 702 Retiree

Gogi Bhandal
United Steelworkers of America,
Vice-President on the Ontario Federation of Labour Board

Ethel Birkett-LaValley
Secretary-Treasurer, Ontario Federation of Labour,
Vice-President representing Aboriginal Peoples, CLC Executive
Council

Sheila Block and Sue Milling
 "Women of Steel" Staff Representatives

Christine Collins
Public Service Alliance of Canada

Muriel Collins
CUPE Local 79

Kathleen Connors, RN
President, Canadian Federation of Nurses' Unions

Pam Constable
Vice-President, Ontario Secondary School Teachers' Federation

Dee Dee Daigle
CLC Representative, Atlantic Region

Judy Darcy
National President, Canadian Union of Public Employees

Debora De Angelis,
United Food and Commercial Workers Union

Tina Eddy
CAW Local 597, St. John's, Nfld.

Sandi Ellis
CLC Regional Representative, Ontario Region

Ivy E. Foye
Canadian Union of Postal Workers

Carol A. Furlong
Secretary-Treasurer of the Newfoundland and Labrador Association
of Public and Private Employees (NUPGE/NAPE)

Natasha Goudar
SFL Youth Coordinator

Heather Grant-Jury
President, Winnipeg Labour Council

Irene Harris
Executive Vice-President, Ontario Federation of Labour

Susan Hart-Kulbaba
Staff Representative, NUPGE/MGEU,
Former Director, Labour Affairs, Crocus Investment Fund,
Former President, MFL

Teresa Healy
Canadian Union of Public Employees

Louisette Hinton
UFCW Canada National Coordinator for Women's Issues

Cheryl Kryzaniwsky
Director – Education Department, CAW–Canada

Peggy Nash
Executive Assistant to the President, CAW–Canada

Winnie Ng
CLC Regional Director, Ontario Region

Lana Payne
FFAW/CAW, St. John's, Newfoundland

Carol Phillips
Director, International Department, CAW–Canada

Elaine Price
President, Newfoundland and Labrador Federation of Labour

Nancy Riche
Secretary-Treasurer, Canadian Labour Congress

Angela Schira
Secretary-Treasurer, B.C. Federation of Labour

Mary Shortall
National Representative, Canadian Labour Congress

Marie St. Aubin
Staff Representative, Canadian Auto Workers

Susan Taylor
Shop Stewart, UFCW Local 1252

Nycole Turmel
National President, Public Service Alliance of Canada

Monica Urrutia
CLC Vice-President for Youth (PSAC)

Foreword

Dear Sisters:

I had an idea (just like Barbara Walters when she conceived of *The View*). Actually, I've had a growing anger over the fact that the mainstream media never seems to recognize (or even see!) the accomplishments of union women.

You know, *Chatelaine* does a piece on successful women: that is, women from business, the financial sector, broadcasting, academia—well, you get the picture. Then one day I opened the book, *Dropped Threads*, and there it was again. "..." So, we contacted women from finance, business and so on, and so on.

"Enough is enough," says I. So I contacted experienced trade union women and asked them to write a letter to a younger trade union sister. I was going to call this collection "Dear Sister." A few months later, at our CLC Women's Committee Retreat, one of those younger sisters said, "Communication is a two-way street!" Of course! And so, I also invited the young sisters to write to us.

And there we have it: *Dear Sister, Dear Sister,* a collection of letters from trade union women (Volume 1?).

Thank you to all who did get their letters in by deadline. To those who didn't, you'll be sorry.

Especially, thank you to Lylia Kuhn, who did all the hard work of tracking down the writers, then doing it again and again. I merely had an idea, Lylia and the CCPA did all the hard work.

But mostly, this book is my gift to all the women in the movement who have supported me, cried with me, laughed with me, and inspired me. You are my best friends. You *are* my sisters.

In Sisterhood and Solidarity,
With love,
Nancy Riche
Trade Union Woman

Dear Sister:

When you ask someone what comes to mind when you say "women and unions," often it's the picture of a diminutive, yet defiant, Norma Rae shutting down a factory with her simple hand-lettered sign spelling "UNION." But behind that Hollywood image is a longer and even more dramatic story, not only of the real Norma Rae, but of women who have struggled for more than a century to secure their rights in the workforce. That hand-printed card said "union," but for women the real meaning behind that word is "respect."

I am an elementary school woman teacher. Women teachers have been in the paid workforce since the 1840s when education came out of the home and into public schools. At the time, women who wanted or needed to work outside the home had few opportunities. We could be domestics, seamstresses, factory workers, nurses, or teachers.

Whatever work we did was by definition "women's work," and therefore paid less than "men's work," even if our toil required more skills. We were paid less even when we did the same or similar work. And we were rarely the bosses, even in workplaces where we were the majority of—or the only—workers.

No woman could ever count on having access to a paying job. Women flooded workplaces in war years, only to be forced out again when the boys came home. Our welcome in the workforce waxed and waned with the economy. During depression years, our jobs were less secure and our wages cut more deeply than those of our brothers. We were expected to make do, be demure, and stay silent about the injustice.

When women elementary teachers argued for equal pay at the beginning of the last century, their school boards offered to accept their resignations if they were so dissatisfied. When our brothers married or fathered children, they were praised for demonstrating responsibility, given bonuses, and even promoted. When we married or became pregnant, we were expected to go home.

At the turn of the century, Miss Lottie Jones, an elementary teacher in Ontario, signed a contract with the following terms: For a salary of $300 a year, she agreed to

- not get married,
- not ride in a carriage or automobile with any man except her brothers or father,
- not leave town without permission,
- not smoke cigarettes or drink beer, wine or whiskey,
- not dye her hair or dress in bright colours,
- wear at least two petticoats,
- keep the school room clean, scrub it with soap and water at least once a week,
- not use face powder, mascara or paint her lips,
- not wear dresses more than two inches above the ankles, and finally
- not loiter downtown in ice cream parlours.★

Men teachers also worked under what now seem ludicrous conditions, but at least they were paid more for their trouble!

To our younger sisters, these stories may seem quaint recountings, like looking at old sepia photographs: perhaps fascinating but ancient history. But it's important to recognize not only how women worked to change our circumstances, but also how much our continued action is important to safeguard our gains.

The history of women in the workforce has been a quest for respect. Respect for women's right to work, and for our right to work when married or pregnant; respect for the work that women do and the value we place on it; and, finally, respect for the circumstances that make women's working lives different from those of our brothers. Women working through and with their unions helped secure that respect.

We now have laws for pay equity and against harassment and discrimination. We have collective agreements that govern our

---

★ Excerpted from *Speak with Their Own Voices*, Pat Staton and Beth Light, FWTAO.

workplaces. These gains, made in the workplace and in society, were not handed down to us by benign male legislators, judges, or bosses. The gains we made were won by our mothers and grandmothers—brave women who banded together, sometimes facing crushing opposition from family, co-workers, and even other women. Unions helped them make those changes.

Women working in coalitions and through their unions, using their collective strength, supported by their union brothers, made the difference. We gained the right to work, pregnancy and parental leaves, family leaves, greater recognition for part-time work, non-discrimination and anti-harassment provisions, pay equity, and more.

So here we are today with the battles won, the rights secured, the pay equal. Unions have done their work and now we can relax. We can all go home and rest on the victories of our predecessors. Right? Wrong!

For women in the workforce, our struggle for respect and recognition is a journey. Our rights are guaranteed on paper and in legislation, but they can be overturned by the stroke of a pen. Security in the workforce is still subject to swings in the economy and shifts in ideology. When governments decide to slash social programs, it's women who are the most severely affected. Cuts to child-care affect working women disproportionately. What was touted as a simple change in Unemployment Insurance entitlements left part-time workers, mostly women, excluded from benefits.

We have made enormous gains, and we have to guard them vigilantly. We have seen what uncaring governments can do to unravel the progress. Complacency is our worst enemy.

Women's lives have their own particular shape. Our working lives are affected by pregnancy and childbirth. Our lives are different because of the responsibilities we take on in society. Women are still the primary care-givers in families, whether for young children or elders. Working women typically have two full-time jobs: one in the workplace and one at home. Women are more likely to have interrupted work histories or to work part-time, and our pensions suffer; many of us face poverty in our old age.

Women are still more vulnerable to violence at home and harassment at work. We are still underrepresented in decision-making positions—in courtrooms, boardrooms, legislatures, and union governing bodies.

All of these factors influence a woman's working life. Decisions, procedures, past practices, even collective agreements that appear gender neutral on the surface, can disadvantage women when applied in the context of women's circumstances in society.

Working in the women's movement through our unions, we must continue the longer-term struggle to change those societal patterns. And until those patterns change, we must work with our unions to ensure that the rules that govern our work lives and our participation reflect the needs we have today.

So what's in it for our brothers? Plenty! When we secure respect for women in our society and in the workplace, we secure respect for all. When penalties and stigma are removed from what have traditionally been known as women's work and women's roles, men will have more options: to work part-time, to stay home with young children, to spend time in their children's school, to take a break without loss of security. Imagine the freedom!

While not ready to retire, I can say I am in the later stages of my career. As a woman teacher and a woman unionist, it's a time for me to reflect, assess, adjust, and, most importantly, think about the legacy I want to leave my younger sisters in the union movement. If I had only one piece of advice to hand down, I would have to make it: Participate in your union! Why? Because that simple action gives you incredible strength. It gives you the power to shape your working life, not have it imposed. It gives women a collective voice that cannot be ignored. It gives you a place in history, cherishing and protecting what your mothers and grandmothers achieved, pushing the envelope to make greater improvements for yourselves and working women who will follow you. We can't trust others to do it for us.

Your participation can take many forms. It can be as simple as informing yourself by reading your union newsletters. You don't even need to leave your home to do that! But do go out: get out to a meeting, become a steward, run for an office. Get involved in community and in social justice issues through your union. You can choose your own personal path in the union. The important thing is to take those first steps.

I am here because the women who preceded me overcame incredible odds to win a place for me as a woman in the workforce. In a way, they took my hand and led me here. Now, take mine and let's continue on the journey.

In Sisterhood and Solidarity,

Phyllis Benedict
President, Elementary Teachers' Federation of Ontario

Dear Sister:

Sisterhood is a mixed blessing! I have laughed, cried, sworn at, and with, fought and apologized, whined and crowed with many women across Canada.

We have shared victories and defeats, strike lines and bread lines, dining, dancing and drinking together, as sisters should. Some great fishing, too!

Countless meetings, hours of debate, endless hours with brothers "who know exactly what should be done," great conferences, seminars, and educationals. Countless miles of travel and more travel (save your toiletries for the local women's shelter).

Mentored by wonderful women who were eagar to share their experience and knowledge. Shunned by others who did not share my values or direction. Some days it seems as though no one loves or understands you, and you really don't know a damn thing about anything! You wonder to yourself, "What am I doing?"

Sister, grab every opportunity you have to take educationals, seminars, discussion groups for women, with women. Take /make the time. The sisters you share with will enrich your life, become friends, and make sisterhood special for you.

Mentor, or be mentored to, whenever you can. Laugh often, cry seldom, brag a little, and always celebrate your contributions and growth in sisterhood.

In Sisterhood and Solidarity,

Ruth Bergman,
Kenora & District Labour Council, Past President
NUPGE/OPSEU Local 702 Retiree

Dear Sister:

My name is Gogi Bhandal and I am a member of Local 9042 of the United Steelworkers of America. I am immensely proud to a member of this great "Everybody's Union." I am a trade unionist, feminist, counsellor, community worker, and a member of a visible minority. I am married with two beautiful children. I was born and raised in India, and came to Canada in 1977.

I have been a member of the Steelworkers since 1985 when my previous union, Upholsters International, merged with Steel. I started my union career in 1979 as a departmental steward and gradually rose through the ranks to become the president of my local. I grew up in the union, because when I became involved in the union I was new in this country. When I joined the union, I could read and write English, but could hardly speak it. I learned to speak English in the union, and the union created a very comfortable environment for me to learn. I had an academic education from India, but the union gave me the "real" education I needed to survive in this country.

During the union education, I was asked to introduce myself, "who I was," and asked to talk about my life and my stories. My union brothers and sisters listened as though it really mattered. I attended many union courses, including a public-speaking course, and learned to chair meetings and host conferences and conventions. Through the union, I have gained education and knowledge in different areas, and as a result of that education I am a Health and Safety Instructor, WSIB Advocate, and Anti-Harassment Counsellor/Facilitator. I am currently serving as a Vice-President on the Ontario Federation of Labour Executive Board.

Union education helped to build my self-esteem and helped me learn "who I am." Getting active in the union and the labour movement has given me a better outlook on life, since the union taught me to stand up for myself, for my members, and the union was always there to help me do that. Without the union I would still be a shy East Indian woman, trapped between home and work.

There are some people in the Steelworkers who have had an immeasurable impact on my success, and it is these people whom I shall remember as my greatest mentors and dear friends.

The union is like a family to me, and I know for a fact that no one can prosper without the love and support of her/his family. My union family has empowered me to prosper and make headway, not only in the union, but in my own home and my community at large. I am being seen in the community as a successful career woman and a source of inspiration to other East Indian women. Within my own family, I have become a role model for my children. My children understand and see the difference unions make in the lives of working people.

I consider myself fortunate to work in a unionized workplace, compared to the thousands of women with whom I speak on a daily basis as part of my current job. I hear them talking about their experiences in non-union workplaces and how badly they are being treated by the management. Studies reveal that women make only 72% of men's incomes in these environments. I see women working for low wages with no benefits. Many have to work two or three jobs with a variety of temporary employment agencies to maintain an adequate standard of living.

Women's wages are essential to the survival of their families. In some cases women are the primary breadwinners. Nearly half are the sole support of their families, and studies suggest that 41% contribute up to half or more than half of their family's total income. Unions have fought for the equality of women and through collective bargaining have reduced that inequality. A union wage is all the more important to families who just depend on the wages of working women for their survival. Therefore, Sisters, we must reach out to the unorganized women to encourage them to join us in the labour movement, so that, like us, they too can enjoy higher wages, better fringe benefits and working conditions, and greater job security.

I know of numerous women who are terrified to talk about unions, because they have been told that "unions are just about strikes and picket lines." We must tell these unorganized women that unions are not about strikes, that unions are a tool for social change, a voice to exercise workers' rights in the workplace against mistreatment and injustice. The standard of living and the quality of life that working people enjoy today came about through the unions' efforts. Unions fought to achieve better pensions, the 40-hour work week, paid vacations, overtime, fringe benefits, equal pay for work of equal value, and improved health and safety. Despite all recent corporate and government efforts to suppress the wages of unionized workers, we still continue to enjoy substantially higher wages than our non-union counterparts.

Many women like myself are serving in the union but still face obstacles to full participation. A recent Steelworkers' survey indicates that women in the union want to increase their level of involvement, and they see the union as an important organization in the struggle for the rights of working families at home and in other parts of the world. We, the visible minority workers, have come a long way and have made important gains in the union and the labour movement as a whole, but not enough. When we look around, we see workers of colour participating in the union more than we did a decade ago, but still we don't see many visible minority members serving as staff and on executive boards, so we need to be much more political in our actions and must get involved in the union to ensure that workers of colour are not only heard, but acted upon.

To achieve what we want, we have to organize the unorganized and educate our people as to why unions are important more than ever. We need unions to help us to stop the exploitation of workers of colour, Aboriginal workers, workers with disabilities, gays and lesbians, and workers in general, and to stop governments' attack on the rights of working people. With more workers organized, we will have more power. A strong labour movement and active union members are the only defence against government and corporations that threaten the livelihood of workers. Despite the attacks by corporations and governments on the unions, I strongly believe that the labour movement remains the most vibrant social force to protect the rights of workers for basic dignity and respect.

In Sisterhood and Solidarity,

Gogi Bhandal
United Steelworkers of America,
Vice-President, Ontario Federation of Labour Board

Dear Sister:

During this time when the economy is down, cellphones continually ringing, laptops busy on planes and at nights in our hotel rooms, forgotten lunches, rushing children out the door to childcare (when we have the luxury of being home), and you feel like getting off this runway we are on, I felt it was important to share some of the Ontario Federation of Labour's history with you.

In 1957, the OFL was comprised of a President, Secretary-Treasurer, and eight Vice-Presidents. In 1958, it was increased to 10 Vice-Presidents. In 1962, it increased to 12 Vice-Presidents. In 1971, the number rose to 14 Vice-Presidents. In 1979, it became 15 Vice-Presidents. In 1981, it became 16 Vice-Presidents. And of course, over all these years, the OFL also had a President and Secretary-Treasurer.

Here's where the action really starts for women.

At the 1982 convention, a Statement on Women and Affirmative Action was adopted, partly committing the OFL to investigate the variety of methods possible to improve the percentage of women on the OFL Executive Board to 30% (in proportion to women's numbers in unions). A subcommittee was struck to examine the options and report back to Convention 1983 with an action plan.

At a special OFL Executive Board meeting on November 21, 1982, a position was taken to place a Notice of Motion before the convention to review the matter of placing five women on the Board, in line with the paper. A subcommittee was struck, and on April 18, 1983, the recommendations of the sub-committee were dealt with.

At the 1983 Convention, five additional Vice-Presidents' seats were allocated to the five largest unions. These seats went to the United Steelworkers of America (USWA), the United Auto Workers (UAW), the Ontario Public Service Employees Union (NUPGE/OPSEU), the United Food and Commercial Workers (UFCW), and the Canadian Union of Public Employees (CUPE). This was done through women organizing and lobbying, with the group Organizing Working Women assisting in effective lobbying, knowing parliamentary procedure, and working the convention floor, and yes, with the help of our brothers in the movement.

In 1986, an Executive Vice-President position was added. In 1987, two new Vice-Presidents' seats were added, one to the UE or CUPW, and one to a visible minority, whose affiliate at the time was not represented. In 1989, another Vice-Presidents' seat was allocated, and then in 1991 an additional seat for a woman was allocated, bringing the total to a President, Secretary-Treasurer, Executive Vice-President, 19 Vice-Presidents, and five additional Vice-Presidents' positions allocated to women.

By 1993, the Officers became President, Secretary-Treasurer, Executive Vice-President, seven Vice-Presidents' seats elected at large allocated to women, two Vice-Presidents elected at large and allocated to visible minority women, 15 Vice-Pesidents elected at large, one Vce-Pesident elected at caucus and allocated to a First Nation person, and one Vice-President elected at caucus to a person with a disability, three Vice-Presidents (one of whom must be a woman) who are Labour Council Presidents.

Today, in 2002, we have gone from election at large to caucus elections for Aboriginal, persons with a disability, gay, lesbian, or bisexual, two Vice-Presidents for visible minorities (at least one of whom must be a woman), one Vice-President allocated to a youth delegate, one Vice-President representing the smallest union voted by caucus, three Labour Council Vice-Presidents (one of whom must be a woman and one who must be from Northern Ontario), 15 largest affiliates' Vice-Presidents, and eight affirmative action Vice-Presidents' positions allocated to women, based on the OFL per capita records for the previous 12 months on each November 1ˢᵗ.

The full-time officers are elected by convention every second year.

Dear Sister, this is the evolution of the Ontario Federation of Labour and the significant role women have played. Today, our executive is 17 female and 15 male.

So when you get tired of the fight, remember those who fought for you and the changes that were made, and remember that the labour movement is counting on you, today's youth, to fly the banner high and proud in support of the sisters before you, and those who will come behind you.

In Sisterhood and Solidarity,

Ethel Birkett-LaValley
Secretary-Treasurer, Ontario Federation of Labour,
Vice-President representing Aboriginal Peoples, CLC Executive Council

Dear Sister:

When you think of the Steelworkers, "Everybody's Union," you probably think about women and men in hard-hats working in heavy industry or mining. Chances are, those men and women are members of our union. But there are some things about our union that might surprise you. One, those workers in heavy industry are standing side by side with thousands of Steelworkers who work in offices, factories, nursing homes, universities, call centres, hotels, airports, credit unions, banks, fish plants, laboratories, and in the transportation sector across the country.

Another thing that might surprise you is that together these men and women are leading the way in developing and implementing policies against harassment, building respectful workplaces, negotiating a balance between work and family responsibilities, and bargaining pay equity.

But all this didn't happen overnight. Many of those sisters and brothers in male-dominated workplaces laid the groundwork. Strong women got and kept jobs in these workplaces and got active in the union, despite all the obstacles in their way. You can imagine it wasn't easy for a woman from Northern Ontario to stand at a convention with hundreds of men and talk about how difficult it was for women to attend conferences when child-care wasn't provided. It wasn't easy, but, thanks in great part to that kind of courage, we now provide child-care at all our conferences and conventions.

In 1990, the Steelworkers were the first union in North America to provide a course for and about women, taught only by women: the Women of Steel Leadership Development Course. After consultations with women of steel, a course was developed and a group of women were brought together to be trained as instructors. Some of the sisters had already been active in the union for over 20 years. A few had experience as instructors and had attended other union events and conferences. Most of the women had gained their experience and expertise outside of the union through community groups or labour councils.

It didn't take long for this group of women to develop a strong bond. After an almost all-night session, or what we now refer to as an historical pyjama party, this group of women realized what potential the women of steel course had to truly open doors for women in the Steelworkers.

For the first time, there was talk about which women activists might become servicing staff representatives and organizers. Many of the first instructors of the Women of Steel course are now on staff or are active organizers and educators in the union. And, to this day, the connections or bonds made during the course are of vital support as women continue to overcome challenges in their workplaces, local unions, and in the community. The "gang of ten" visible minority sisters who attended the first women of steel course held for women of colour only in the late 1990s continue to work together to encourage other women of colour to get active in the union.

The Women of Steel course was the catalyst for a number of changes in the union. It led to active womens' committees in locals and helped to establish and strengthen District Womens' Committees. The District 6 (Ontario) Womens' Committee, active for a number of years prior to the course, held regular womens' conferences. The course helped to increase the participation in those conferences, activities and programs of the union.

In 1995, National Director Lawrence McBrearty established a National Women's Committee. A year later, at the end of 1996, the union held its first national womens' conference. It is hard to describe the energy and excitement in the air of that conference. For many of us, it was the first time that we had been at a union event where women were anything more than a tiny minority. We realized that we aren't alone in our struggles. These conferences energize our activists and provide them with the tools they need when they go back to their locals.

Many women join unions because they are looking for dignity and respect at work. They also expect it from their union. In the late 1980s, our union faced and addressed a major incident of harassment at a workplace. It wasn't the first incident of harassment a union member had faced, but we are particularly proud of our leadership's response to it. The union decided that no woman should have to face that kind of harassment again without the support of the union. The Steelworkers developed an anti-harassment policy for all union events and activities. Almost 15 years later, Steelworker meetings and events begin with reading out the statement, known throughout the union as the "yellow sheet." It clearly states that harassment strikes at the heart of union solidarity.

In the early 1990s, the union developed an anti-harassment workplace training program. We trained a group of local union instructors who reflect the diversity of the union. Well over 35,000 Steelworkers have now participated in workplace sessions.

Fear of harassment is still noted as the No. 1 barrier to participation by women and visible minority persons. We are always looking for ways to improve our practices and procedures to ensure we are "walking the talk." Again, it isn't easy and we depend on a network of trained anti-harassment counsellors, as well as the workplace training facilitators, to help make sure that we are doing what we can to prevent and deal with harassment.

The Steelworkers has also taken on women's economic issues, including our 40-year-old tradition of job evaluation. The union found that our job evaluation system did not meet the requirements of pay equity legislation, so, we developed a new gender-neutral system. SES, a Simple Effective Solution to Pay Equity and Job Evaluation, is now used in a wide variety of workplaces. Not only does SES help make job requirements in women's jobs visible, but the process also helped to bring women onto workplace job evaluation and negotiating committees. Pay equity was benefiting pay cheques and helping to change the face of the union.

The third national women's conference in 2001 again broke new ground. Focusing on bargaining, the conference provided women with skills, resources, and confidence to get involved in the bargaining process and bring women's issues to the bargaining table.

Another key priority for our women's committees is to work in coalition with the women's movement and with our political allies. In the last federal election, we had a record number of Women of Steel run as candidates for the New Democratic Party. Each year, Steelworkers organize events on International Women's Day, the International Day for the Elimination of Racism, and Pride Days. We continue to work alongside our union and community sisters on the demands of the World March of Women to end poverty and violence against women.

Despite all we have achieved, Women of Steel still have to deal with the potential for backlash. Especially in tough times, we fight to maintain gains we have made, to make sure women are represented at all levels of unions, and to nurture and train women activists. We need to work as hard as ever in the union and workplace to help women balance work and family responsibilities, and to support each other in our work. There are still some members who believe that Women of Steel want something different from Men of Steel, that our committees, conferences and workshops, once important, are no longer necessary. Again, we have only to look to the organizing successes and gains the union has made over the last 10 years to see what a tremendous difference our "special" and unique initiatives have made to the union.

Women of Steel are very proud Steelworkers. The confidence and support of our sisters and brothers in continuing to reach out and find new and better ways to involve more women in the union can only help to build a stronger union, and a stronger labour and social democratic movement in Canada.

So when you see someone in a Women of Steel sweatshirt or wearing a Women of Steel button, or hear someone humming or singing the Women of Steel song from our CD, know that, while there is always more to do, we have come a long way together.

Our most successful organizing—in universities, call centres, and security guards—is a credit to the union's strong tradition on bargaining and defending our members. It is also a testament to the hard work of our sisters and brothers over the years who have carried on and strengthened a commitment and tradition of fighting for equality, of fighting for a union that can truly call itself "Everybody's Union."

In Sisterhood and Solidarity,

Sheila Block and Sue Milling
 "Women of Steel" Staff Representatives

P.S.—If you want a "Women of Steel" pin or a copy of our CD, or any of the policies referred to, contact us through our web site at www.uswa.ca

Dear Sister:

If I could pass on anything to you that I have learned during my more than 20 years as a trade union activist, I think it would be to tell you to never give up if you believe in your cause.

As a PSAC woman who was very involved in our long struggle for pay equity, I would like to share some of the ups and downs along the way. The most important aspect is that I, along with many of our sisters, believed from the onset that we would achieve victory, although none of us thought it would take 15 long years. I do not recall even one instance that I doubted that we would win.

I first became involved in this struggle in the early stages. I was one of the PSAC members selected by my union to work on the joint Union-Management Pay Equity Study. At the time, it seemed like a very long year! Our work consisted of trying to evaluate positions as part of a committee that was comprised of management representatives, other union representatives, and our PSAC representatives—a tough job, one could say. We did, however, manage to get the job done and, although there were a few rough times, overall everyone on the committees agreed with the majority of the work completed.

Then came the first major problem. Treasury Board took a look at the results of our work and the cost to implement equal pay for work of equal value within the federal government, and unilaterally decided to ignore the study results and pay only a pittance to their clerical and secretarial employees. Following this action, our complaint was then heard by a government-appointed tribunal. In the end, after what seemed to be too many years, the tribunal ruled in our favour on most aspects, and ordered pay equity to be implemented and interest paid back to 1985.

The federal government, however, then decided to appeal this ruling to the Federal Court that, in turn, again after what seemed like a very long time (but in reality was probably the shortest of all our waits) ruled in our favour again. A settlement was finally reached a little more than two years ago, and most of our members now get equal pay for work of equal value in their workplace. The struggle continues, however, for our members who are now in the private sector.

I do not believe we would have achieved this historic victory if we had not been active in keeping this issue as a priority throughout the years with our employer, with the public, and with our union. Treasury Board used many different tactics during this period to try to split our membership. One such tactic was to make a public offer through the media of a percentage of what was owed, with a "take-it-or-it's-gone" theme; other tactics included publicizing a claim that paying pay equity would be a burden on the taxpayers—and on and on and on.

Over the years, we kept up the pressure on the government with many different actions: occupations of Ministers' offices; demonstrations; letter-writing and postcard campaigns; a campaign of invoicing the government for monies owed and, on the 13th anniversary, we held a 13-hour, 13-women vigil. We sent balloon-o-grams to Liberal Party members; visited constituency offices; lobbied for pay equity as part of the NAC's annual lobby of Parliament.

PSAC women spoke at numerous events on pay equity; we took every opportunity to speak to the media and to put faces to our fight; we held workshops to educate our own members on the issue, as well as other actions that I have probably long forgotten. One highlight and a great memory that I will have always was our "Pay Equity Eleven" and our occupation of the Office of the Minister of State for the Status of Women. Even when we were arrested some 14 hours later, we tried to negotiate with the arresting officers to have women arrest us and highlighted the need for more women police officers.

As important to me were the friends that were made during this time: some sisters that I will never forget although we rarely meet any longer. And of course, most important, we never gave up.

In closing, involvement in the labour movement can be most rewarding in friendships formed, allies gained, and being part of a wonderful support network.

Do get involved.

In Sisterhood and Solidarity,

Christine Collins
Public Service Alliance of Canada

Dear Sister:

This is my story as a union sister.

I will try to share with you my experiences as a worker in the struggles to end racism and sexism and all inequities for women in the workplace.

I am a retired health care worker. I belong to CUPE Local 79, a large local representing workers at Toronto City Hall, Riverdale Hospital, and Toronto Homes for the Aged. The majority of our members are women.

The union's fight for full-time jobs, pay equity, and employment equity has always been practical and straightforward when bargaining with employers who really thought our demands were a joke. The things we worked for and achieved have benefited not only our members, but our whole community.

I worked in solidarity with other women—my sisters in other unions within and also outside Canada. I talked with them about the need to stick together in spite of employers' efforts to divide us. I talked about the need to encourage people to stand together for our rights.

We know in our hearts that racism and sexism divide us. We need to put an end to cheap remarks that pit Black against White, Italians against Filipinos, men against women, straights against gays, worker against worker.

Do you know about our fight for things that meet the needs of workers: pensions, maternity benefits, parental leave, flex-time, co-op housing, and child care? Do you know how we gained protections in the face of resistance from employers and the right wing? All these things the house of labour fought for and defended.

Many years ago, on the day the Supreme Court issued the Morgentaler decision, I was in Ottawa, attending a CLC women's conference. It was thrilling to be with so many sisters on that victorious day. We marched in joy together to the steps of the Supreme Court.

Sisters, let us look beyond ourselves. Know that solidarity with our sisters struggling in developing countries is an essential part of our commitment to build a peaceful, economically secure, and equal world.

Dear Sisters! There is still much more to accomplish. Let us work together for change.

Rise, sisters, rise.

We still have many rivers to cross.

Be proud. Hold your banner high.

In Sisterhood and Solidarity,

Muriel Collins
Retiree of CUPE Local 79

Dear Sister:

I wasn't always a "professional" in the eyes of the medical establishment. Sure, I'm a registered nurse with 30 years of specialized training and clinical practice. Like most nurses, I've made life-and-death judgments and saved lives. I've been there to help newborns take their first breath. And I've been there when the last heartbeat ended a life. But that didn't cut much mustard in the not-so-old days.

Then doctors and health administrators treated nurses like hired help at best, and as indentured servants a lot of the time.

How were they able to do that? The doctors and the bosses used a number of techniques to manipulate you into subservience. They told us, "You're professionals, dedicated to your patients! Your dedication and compassion means you are selfless—an example to us all."

There was something about caring implied in those words that sounded good. In reality, they meant, "We get the pay, the credit, the prestige. And you nurses get the privilege of doing what we tell you." Our education also contributed to our subservience. In fact, the motto of the first Canadian school of nursing was, "I see and I am silent."

But we are silent no more.

When we organized our sister nurses into labour unions, that began to change—at least for some, initially, and for a lot more later.

The first to heed labour's call were the bold. Something in them made it possible to say, "I can see through the prairie-grass-land-pie you're serving up, Mister. You can eat it yourself."

For those few with what seemed like innate common sense and vision, strength in numbers made instant perfect sense. But for others, it took longer. The words of the MDs and the bosses rang in their ears: "Do you want to be a common worker? You are a professional. Don't get down there with them."

The organizers fought back. We said, "Don't listen to what they say. Look at what they do. The words are nice, but do they really respect your skills, your insight, and your intuition? Do they ask for your opinion or only your silent compliance?"

But it required more than reason. Convincing many nurses to join the movement required an understanding of the motivation behind nursing. It required us to point out that, as nurses, we couldn't best advocate for and protect our patients unless we were full partners in health care.

What happened at the Winnipeg Health Sciences Centre Pediatric Cardiac Care Unit in the 1990s reminds me of the stories we'd regularly hear before nurses' unions existed.

In Winnipeg, nurses repeatedly pointed out that a surgeon there was putting the lives of their little patients at risk. In fact, babies died and nurses took risks to warn authorities inside and outside the hospital about it. Why outside? A justice of the Manitoba Supreme Court found that the concerns of nurses were "casually dismissed" by doctors and health administrators.

No one was actually fired for attempting to blow the whistle. In the not-so-distant pre-union bad old days, they would have been fired and blacklisted, to be more precise.

In those organizing days, we pointed out that the union would provide protection so that nurses could stand up for patients and health care workers. More respect, better pay, and greater freedom to stand up for patients sounded good, and the nurses' union movement grew.

By the way, the women who organized these unions, like their counterparts in all other kinds of work, risked big. And they won big.

Today there are 122,000 nurses in CFNU unions—96% of them women. While it is still risky to tell a doctor or a health administrator that his or her incompetence is jeopardizing patients' lives, it happens because women are brave and the union stands behind them.

But remember, it started with those women who got it the first time. It started with those women who believed in solidarity, who believed enough, who were brave enough, to risk their careers.

People are alive today because of them. Health care is better because of them.

Every nurse you meet, whether she knows it or not, can enjoy her elevated status because she is standing on the shoulders of the nurses and the other men and women in the labour movement who organized despite the threats.

They are among Canada's true heroes.

My advice to you is to search for the hero in you—if you haven't already found her. Your sisters and brothers need her. Canada needs her, too. She's there. Good luck.

In Sisterhood and Solidarity,

Kathleen Connors, RN
President, Canadian Federation of Nurses' Unions

Dear Sister:

I was recently involved with a 14-week-long strike in northwestern Ontario. It was the longest strike ever for the OSSTF and involved education assistants and office, clerical and library technicians in a school board (about 200 women and three men).

Going on strike was the last thing we wanted to do, but in negotiations we kept banging up against a long-entrenched attitude on the other side of the table about the value of women's work. The employer had slashed the workers' hours and cut back benefits. As I watched the bargaining and the attitudes at the table, I realized I was witnessing an abusive relationship. I make this comparison reluctantly, but it is accurate. The employer would ignore the collective agreement, take away the women's rights, kick them around emotionally, but on the other hand say that they really did appreciate the employees' work and how important they were to the schools and children. It was like watching someone get hit and then being told they were loved, so please stay. Well, we didn't stay. We walked and we walked for 14 weeks.

I learned a lot from my sisters on the picket line. They learned a lot about each other and themselves. While picketing on minus-38-degree Celsius mornings and in meetings later in the day, we talked about finding the strength to stand for what's right. The employer had told people to watch and wait—that the women would eventually "crumble" and limp back to work. That infuriated our members to no end. One actually said, "I'd rather be dipped in shit than go back under their terms." That statement received thunderous applause from the other strikers.

We learned that others do care about what happens to people. Other unions, retired people, community groups, parents, and neighbours brought us food, coffee, money—and support in a hundred ways. It was clear to us that cutting back services to kids was not supported in the community and that we were right to put an end to it. We learned we could laugh even under extreme financial pressure. We learned we could count on each other to buoy our spirits and shore up our resolve.

The strike ended, the bargaining unit members got back much of what they lost. What the members won for each other and themselves was self-respect and a recognition that they have power. I've been involved in the labour movement for many years. What I got the most from being with this amazing, strong and resilient group of women was the confirmation of what can be achieved when we stand together, and that there is strength in solidarity. This is the gift that the union movement gives to women workers.

In Sisterhood and Solidarity,

Pam Constable
Vice-President, Ontario Secondary School Teachers' Federation

Dear Sister:

If I have any profound words to pass on, it would be: *never give up.*

When I think of all the gains women have made over the centuries, it's because they never gave up trying to change things. No matter what adversaries they faced, they just kept going.

My first personal experience was with a sister I worked with at the telephone company in Saint John, N.B. Roberta was the shop steward for the operators, and she signed me up as a union member after my probationary period. I became a member of the IBEW. She also arranged to drive me to my first local union meeting. This may not sound like a big deal, but she had to drive from the north end of the city to the south end to get me, then to the west side for the meeting, and then reverse the procedure after the meeting.

I can still remember how I felt when we walked into that room— the only women there. At that time, the operators and repair/installation workers were all in one local. Of course the operators were all women and the repair/installation workers were all men at that time. We're talking 1972, so it's not that ancient in historical terms.

I wasn't sure I belonged there—didn't know what was going on— and sure had no idea what parliamentary procedure was all about. I remember the meeting and how the discussions centred around the issue of washroom facilities when the "guys" were out in the field. I was completely lost.

Roberta's help in explaining things to me as the meeting unfolded has always stayed with me. I have tried to help other union members who are "new" when I know it's their first meeting, conference or convention, because of the assistance I received from her.

Towards the end of the meeting—under what I now know to be "New Business"—Roberta said that she would be making a motion and she wanted me to "second" it; she would let me know when it was time. Her motion was that the local "establish a separate local for the operators." Of course, no one but me was willing to second this motion. I can still remember the points she raised: the women needed our own contract, our own union meetings, opportunity to discuss our issues, our own representatives at labour council, etc. Needless to say, the motion was defeated. We were the only two who voted "yes."

On the drive home, I said that it was a shame she didn't get what she had wanted. Her reply was that she had been doing this at meetings for over two years now—trying to get a separate local for the women operators. I was stunned and amazed that someone would keep trying and repeatedly getting defeated. Her words to me were: "If any woman who fought to improve things gave up after her first defeat, or even her fifty-first, we would still not even have the right to vote. Women can never give up fighting for what we know to be right and just."

Roberta finally succeeded a few months later in getting a separate local, and, of course, she was the first president of that local. Her commitment and courage to "never give up" has always been an example for me, and for other women, to continue the struggle for equality and justice for all women.

So my words of wisdom to pass on to you are: don't give up! Don't let temporary setbacks stop you. Victories—large and small—will come if we persevere.

We need you to keep fighting—not just for us seniority-challenged women, but also for your generation and the generations to come.

In Sisterhood and Solidarity,

Dee Dee Daigle
CLC Representative, Atlantic Region

Dear Sister:

This letter is for you, our young women activists, who hold the future of the labour movement in your hands and in your hearts.

I was 23 when I first got involved in my union. I was running a photocopy machine at the University of Toronto library. The blinding, flashing lights were giving us workers massive headaches and—even though part-timers weren't organized then—the union went to bat for us and we got sunglasses to protect our eyes. A victory for the right to health and safety on the job.

So I was hooked on the idea that workers, through their collective power, could move the boss to act before I was even in the union. And when I started a full-time job, I became a union steward before my probation was up—and I was local union president two years later.

If your first experience as an activist is anything like mine was, you're probably finding the labour movement a pretty exciting, but also sometimes a frustrating place. That unions can be a positive force for change in our workplaces and our communities is really exciting. The frustrating part for us as activists is that change is sometimes too slow. Or worse, that two steps forward is followed by one step, or even two, backwards.

Take what's happening right now in our country: the massive attempt by the right to drag workers backwards. They want to take us back to the days before public health care, the days when women had few options but to be unpaid caregivers working in the home, the days when workers were forced to rely on the benevolence and good-will of their employers to get a raise, the days when you had to quit your job if you were going to have a child. Back to those "Happy Days," which like the old TV sit-com had nothing to do with workers' reality. Or women's reality.

I remember those 'happy days' in the labour movement. When I brought my four-month-old son with me to a CLC Convention in 1984 and a brother asked me, 'What's more important to you, anyway? Your baby or your union.' I was so stunned—and overwhelmed by guilt—that I didn't think to ask him whether he had put the same question to male delegates at the convention.

That we have child-care offered at today's union gatherings is now taken for granted. Yes, we still have sexism. Now it's usually subtler, but we've learned to see it for what it is. And we've learned to share our experiences so together we can challenge sexism (and racism and other forms of discrimination) in the workplace and in our union.

What I do remember about my early days of activism in CUPE Local 1230 was how exhilarating that experience was. I still feel incredibly lucky to have become part of a union like CUPE where a young worker, a brand new member, is able to jump into the local union with both feet and feel they can get involved and make a difference. Then, it took time for us to learn that we had power as women to make gains. That we had power as members to make change in our union. We had to build our confidence and work together.

The young CUPE women I meet today—who work in child-care, women's shelters, health care, schools, universities, libraries and municipalities—really do inspire me. Your willingness to stand up and fight, to say no, and to demand respect for the work you do is awesome. And today, more then ever, the union movement needs young workers who are willing to dream. Young women who are willing to lead.

Today CUPE's ranks are more than 60% women, and more than half of our local unions are led by women. I am honoured to be the second woman to be President of CUPE. The ground ahead of me was paved by Grace Hartman, who was elected in 1975. Grace was not only the first woman to become leader of a national union, she was the first major union leader to put equality issues on the bargaining table.

Our National Women's Committee was created more than two decades ago. Our national Equality Branch today works not just with union women, but workers of colour, Aboriginal workers, gay and lesbian workers, and workers with disabilities. These activists help ensure that we engage all members in our union, and that we reach out and engage workers in our communities—to take on the closing of women's shelters and hospital beds, the cutbacks to home care and child-care, the growing violence and racism, the over-crowded, dirty classrooms, the issue of safe, clean water for our families to drink.

Today, more than ever, with young workers being bombarded into believing that unions are about protecting "special interests," it's important to get out the message: *we are our communities.*

The battles we're fighting are about *people's* rights: workers' rights, women's rights, and young peoples' rights.

Nowhere is that more clear than in Mike Harris's/Ernie Eves's Ontario, Ralph Klein's Alberta—and now especially in Gordon Campbell's British Columbia where, with a few strokes of the leg-islative pen, they are wiping out jobs by the thousands, stripping workers of their hard-won rights, and rolling back gains for women that took literally decades to achieve.

It's no coincidence that the same governments that are closing women's shelters are also rolling back pay equity and attacking un-ions. Without economic independence, women can't walk away from violence in their homes. Without shelters, women have no-where to go. Without unions, we wouldn't have made gains in wages and benefits, on maternity leave, parental leave, harassment, and employment equity.

The issues that women put on the public agenda and the union agenda in the 1970s and 1980s have been put on the bargaining table across the country. These are the gains they're rolling back when they tear up our collective agreements. This is what's at stake when they say they can't afford to pay us what we're worth. As women, we can't afford anything less.

Nor can you as a young woman worker. The attack on the public sector, which is over 70% unionized, is an attack on present and future jobs for women. Every job that's eliminated is a job that will never exist for a young person. As well, the jobs that are disap-pearing are the better paying jobs for women. The struggle we're waging today is as much about women's economic health and the future of our youth as it is about choosing to keep Medicare public, protecting our fresh water supplies, and deciding what kind of society we want to live in.

The point I want to make is that it *is* possible to make change in your working life—and yes, in our society—by getting involved in the union. The key ingredients to success are: reaching out and involving our union members, mobilizing our communities, being prepared to stand up and fight, and sustaining the fight for months and even years, if that's what it takes.

It is *also* possible to make change in your union. The key is sticking by your principles, sticking it out, and learning how to work with others to make change happen. Whether it's a women's committee, a rainbow caucus, a youth committee, an action caucus, a local union executive, a National Executive Board, or whatever, you can't get very far shaking things up on your own. And you sure as hell can't deal with the frustrations and the barriers and the sexism or the racism all on your own. You shouldn't even try!

There have been important changes in the labour movement since I first got involved. There are more women and young people and workers of colour on union executives and on union staff than there were 10 years ago, much less 30 years ago. There's a growing recognition that unions must focus on mobilizing members and mobilizing communities in order to make real change.

There's a recognition on the part of many—but certainly not all—that the labour movement must work with broad coalitions of social justice groups if we're going to achieve our goals. The labour movement today is an incredibly exciting place to live and work. Now, I'm not going to try to tell you that everything's hunky dory, and that the walls in the labour movement have all come down. You wouldn't believe me if I did! The truth is that it's still tough to *become* a union leader if you're a woman—and it's a whole lot tougher if you're an Aboriginal person, or a person with a disability, or if you're gay or lesbian, or if you're black.

It's also still tough to *be* a woman union leader. The "old boys' club" and the sexist stereotypes are still alive and well. I could write a book about that, but since this is a letter, I'll have to cut it short. For now, let me just say, there *are* more women in leadership positions in the Canadian labour movement than ever before—and collectively we refuse to be type-cast or pushed aside.

Is it still a struggle? Absolutely.

Is it worth it? You bet it is.

There is no other institution—no other place in our society—where workers, where young people, where women, are able to take control over their futures and improve their lives.

There is no other place in our society where workers can become leaders and realize their full potential by making social change. I believe that with all my heart.

Solidarity Forever isn't just a song we sing at union gatherings; it's a declaration of what binds us together as a movement.

The union is a place to stand. A place to grow. A place to fight for all workers, here and across the globe. It's your place, too. As the line on that old button says: A Woman's Place *is* in her Union!

In Sisterhood and Solidarity,

Judy Darcy
National President, Canadian Union of Public Employees

Dear Sister:

I'm a young union activist. Well, I'm not that young any more (I'm 27), but I got involved in the labour movement when I was young—19, to be exact. I saw and experienced injustice in my workplace and fought against it by organizing it. I've been active in the union movement ever since.

The labour movement was a strange place for me in the beginning, and sometimes it still is. Sometimes I find it too political, in the sense that it appears that too many people are jostling for very few positions. I'm uncomfortable with this competition and culture, which only seems to drain our energies rather than renew and strengthen them.

In the beginning, I was fortunate to have a woman (okay, a "sister") who made space for me and took me under her wing. She taught me how to make my way around this movement, to freely say what I believe, and never look back. And there were others, like the women at conventions, some I didn't even know, who would smile and encourage me to go to the microphone and have my voice heard. Later I would see these women applauding. They were there at OFL Executive Board meetings, teaching me how it all worked. And they were there in my workplace, counselling me and warning me about what would get me into trouble and what wouldn't. I owe it to those women and the women in my work life today who still watch out for me, and make sure I don't make any serious mistakes.

What I've learned the most from these courageous women is how to share information and make space for others. They've taught me that there's too much work out there for only one of us. We need as many young women involved in this movement as possible. They've taught me that the movement doesn't move forward if we hog information instead of sharing it. I've used these lessons, and I share these lessons daily with the young people who work with me to make this movement as inclusive and awesome as it can be. This culture of sharing and solidarity versus the culture of competition should be what we strive for in order to strengthen our movement.

I'm really lucky that there were women in the movement who were willing to mentor me. For women out there in the movement who want to make a difference, take a young woman today under your wing. Leave her space to be creative, and remember there are many ways of doing the same thing, so don't be upset if she doesn't always follow what you've suggested.

We understand that we have lots to learn from your generation, but our generation has some neat things to share with you as well. Mind you, sometimes the way we do things is very different, but this is where we need the space, and your support. I hear the frustration from women in the movement when our generation does things that may seem like we're not supporting the struggles and battles the women's movement achieved. Your generation opened the doors for us to be here, and we appreciate it and realize it every time we do the same job as our male co-worker and get paid the same, or when we have a baby and get to enjoy maternity leave, or when we return from maternity leave and our jobs are still there for us. Now it is our job to make it possible for the next generation of women to "have it all."

Something that lots of young women struggle with is the issue of balance, and balance is something that I'm personally having a difficult time with. How do I continue to be an activist, and yet have a family, a social life, and not lose all my friends outside of this movement? How do I take time out to have a family, and not feel guilty about it? Your generation has struggled longer than we have with the issue of balancing work, social life, and your family. Teach us how to balance and not burn out.

So, to all the women in the labour movement who are reading this letter, a sincere thanks for your struggles and battles which have made the world we live in today a much better place.
Thanks for all the women who take the time to share their experiences, information and wise words with us. And a personal thanks to you, Nancy, for the path you've charted for us, on the occasion

of your retirement I ask that you stay in touch and continue to guide us into the future.

In Sisterhood and Solidarity,

Debora De Angelis,
United Food and Commercial Workers Union

Dear Sister:

I am a 27-year-old union activist. I have been working in a unionized environment for most of the 10 years of my employment. I have always had an interest in the way unions work because my father has been working in a unionized environment for a number of years. I didn't really catch the bug until I started working within a government department in Newfoundland and realized to a great extent what the union can provide. I received overwhelming encouragement from my co-workers (who were mostly twice my age) to become involved in the labour movement. The president of the local was a woman at the time, and that's what sealed the deal. I can't thank her enough.

Wow! What an eye-opener, to attend the meetings on a regular basis, serving as Shop Steward, attending conventions and training. It really makes you aware of how much activity is involved in unions and the labour movement. But my knowledge and extent of the labour movement was still minimal, so I decided to take a distance education course in Labour Studies (paid for by my local, of course; God love them). I had no idea how hard the early trade unionists had worked and how much they had to sacrifice to bring us to this point today. Not many people do, especially the youth today. It gave me a profound appreciation for our benefits today and how they were reached.

I would like to express my gratitude, not only to the women who struggled in the 19th and 20th centuries, but to those who are still struggling today to ensure that we retain our benefits and every aspect of good living that comes with the labour movement. I am also proud to say that I am one of those women now who not only struggles for every woman in the movement, but for the youth of today who need our guidance and support—for they are the ones who will have to continue the battle tomorrow.

In Sisterhood and Solidarity,

Tina Eddy
CAW Local 597, St. John's, Nfld.

Dear Sister:

Let me begin by telling you how much I admire your Vitality, Energy and Enthusiasm (that spells VEE for victory). You have it, I know you do. I remember having so much of it ten or twenty years ago! But it seems to recede somewhat after age 45, when mid-life and menopause bring mind-bending changes.

I vividly recall wanting to "Change the World!" I've since settled on attempting to change the world, one person at a time. Obviously my work will never be done in my lifetime or yours.

That word "change" fills so much of our conscious world these days. We hear of "change agents," "the changing workplace," "technological change," "the changing global market." McDonalds restaurants used to brag they were places where you could get "change for a change" (could be indicative of the food served there).

Not all change is good or necessary. But the changes women have made in the history of our world have brought us forward by leaps and bounds. These were society-altering, empowering changes made for the betterment of all, not just a few.

This has been done through baby first steps, one at a time. And you, too, will have your own personal first steps to reflect upon as you grow into old age.

My own firsts include:
- being one of the first female letter carriers ever hired in my city,
- starting the "Senior Citizens Alert Program" to keep an eye on and care about the seniors who live on any one mail route,
- co-ordinating the first years of the "Letters to Santa" program in my city,
- being the first ever person Canada Post in my city "loaned" to United Way for an eight-week campaign period,
- being the first union executive member that a management person had ever nominated for a Silver Postmark Award in my city
- being the first ever labour person nominated for an Oktoberfest "Woman of the year" award,

- being the first ever woman elected municipally to the local hydro commission (previously viewed as an eternal "old boys" club),
- being the first ever non-Mayor Chairperson of that hydro commission,
- being the first person hired as a Labour Staff Representative at a local United Way, and
- being among the first female Regional Staff Reps hired in Ontario by the Canadian Labour Congress.

These were not "world-changing" giant steps, but ones that made a difference in my community and ones of which I am very proud.

There have been many women throughout our feminist history who have sacrificed and paid the price to push forward the rights of women. Mother Theresa, of course, comes to mind, but the women in the labour movement and in political life never get their due admiration: Nellie McClung, Grace Hartman, Audrey McLaughlin, and so many more you should read and learn about.

They had to forge ahead through incredible backlash, including going to jail. But they persisted. We now walk the path they created, wearing and widening it until it becomes a highway down which we can speed.

And whether we are "Women of Steel" in the United Steelworkers, or "Women of the CEP" in the Communications, Energy and Paperworkers Union, or a "Sister from Hell" (an off-the-wall name chosen by a group of sisters in the Canadian Union of Postal Workers), or a member of the Canadian Auto Workers' "Women's network," or a member of a Women's Committee of a Labour Council, or part of any other labour or union women's group or committee, we must always believe that together we can make our workplaces, our communities, and our world a better place to be for all.

We are then truly SISTERS IN SOLIDARITY.

In Sisterhood and Solidarity,

Sandi Ellis
CLC Regional Representative, Ontario Region

Dear Sister:

I would like to provide you, a young trade union sister, with my personal history of how and why I became so intensely involved in my union, the Canadian Union of Postal Workers, and this movement.

When I started working for Canada Post and was a CUPW sister, I was 23 years old and I knew virtually nothing about unions and their function. But, having been involved in CUPW as my first introduction to organized labour, I have come to know CUPW as the most pure and idealistic union, in my humble opinion.

I soon learned a few tough lessons in those early years. Some fellow brothers felt I was taking away "a man's job" by being hired by the Post Office. At that time, I was one of only two women in an office of 12. I quickly became initiated into the trials and tribulations of being a woman in a "man's world," and I developed a toughness and ability to stand my ground that has held me in good stead ever since.

Besides being newly hired, I was pregnant and had to hide that fact until my six-month probation period expired, for fear of being let go. Even at that young age, I realized my employer cared about profits and results over workers' rights, and my union soon taught me who *really* supported women's issues and women's rights!

In 1981, while I was still on Unemployment Insurance maternity benefits, the "Posties" went on strike, with one of their key demands being paid maternity leave. Here was a union of predominately men across the county, willing to walk the streets for 42 days to achieve paid maternity leave, *and then won it*! What a revelation for me. CUPW led the way for all other unions across the country to bargain for paid maternity leave.

Sister, I have to admit I was naive at times to believe everything would run smoothly with my involvement in the union movement, but there are ups and downs in all facets of our lives. As long as the ups outweigh the downs, get involved, stay involved, and help your sisters and brothers along the way. You'll "get it" when you get it.

One of my key inspirations was a short chance meeting with a brother who represents the epitome of what CUPW is all about: Jean-Claude Parrot, the then President of CUPW. In my early union years, I was scheduled to appear before a Liberal government Task Force on Harassment and Intimidation in the Post Office. Being a new employee/activist/mother, I was naturally fearful for my career and the prospect of speaking publicly in a televised formal setting. By chance, in my ride in the elevator to the event, Jean Claude was there, introduced himself, and, when he heard of my nervousness and where I was heading, he gave me wise words, which I use every time I need them. He merely said, "You'll be fine, Sister! When you speak from the heart, you can't go wrong." I did just that, and I have practised and benefited from those sage words ever since.

Sister, I encourage you to attend union educationals, learn the history of the labour movement and the women's rights struggles, and arm yourself with the knowledge and commitment you will need to represent and serve your sisters and brothers. Because of the hard work and dedication of those who have gone before us, there are lots of opportunities for sisters like yourself to win elections at your local, regional, and national labour bodies. I started out as vice-president of a local of 12 members, and, with the support of my sisters and brothers, today I am proud to serve them as Secretary-Treasurer of the Nova Scotia Federation of Labour, sit on the Canadian Labour Congress National Women's Committee, serve as secretary of our Labour Council in Cape Breton, etc., etc.

A natural question to ask yourself as you proceed down the path of trade unionism is: "Do I, or can I make a difference?" I'll tell you, from my perspective, that as the old Chinese saying goes, "every great journey begins with little steps," and I assure you, as Brother Parrot once assured me, that, "when you go with your heart, you can't go wrong!"

I have had my share of ups and downs, as most people do, but I can attest to the fact that the rewards are worth the hard work, dedication, and commitment that the labour and women's movements can call for. I hope these few words will give you insight and inspiration, and I pray that the fact that you've taken the time to read this letter will motivate you to join in the struggle.

In Sisterhood and Solidarity,

Ivy E. Foye
Canadian Union of Postal Workers

Dear Sister:

The political arena can be a tough place for anyone. Women, however, seem to have an even more difficult time getting elected to key positions, and the union environment is no different. The world of politics, without a doubt, has been a man's domain, run and controlled by the "old boys' club." Every now and again women manage to break down those barriers. But it is not easy. Those of us who have broken through the barriers have done so with much adversity and on a regular basis have to jump over hurdles that men do not often encounter.

There is a disproportionate ratio of women politicians to men. There are very few women in key elected positions in the labour movement, or in federal or provincial politics. Only one woman rose to the top of the Canadian political scene to become Prime Minister, and she was ousted after only a few months. There has only been one female Premier in the whole country. Women comprise only 20% of elected representatives in the House of Commons.

These figures are a stark reflection of women's inequality in the political ranks. The labour movement is consistent with other levels of politics. Shirley Carr is the only female to have the privilege of being elected President of the Canadian Labour Congress. Nancy Riche, Secretary-Treasurer of the CLC, is currently its only full-time female officer. In public sector unions, the vast majority of the membership is comprised of females, yet males dominate the top jobs. CUPE is an aberration, with females (until recently) in both top positions. PSAC, NUPGE/OPSEU, and NUPGE/NSGEU are a few of the larger public sector unions with women Presidents, while NUPGE/BCGEU and NUPGE/NAPE have women in the second top position.

When I decided to run, there were two issues I had to deal with. One was that the election of the President and the Secretary-Treasurer was for the first time to be by a full membership vote, as opposed to a few hundred delegates at a convention, so this involved a new method of campaigning. Secondly, no woman had ever been elected to a top paid position within NUPGE/NAPE.

In my own experience, I had tremendous support from female members, but I also received the same support and encouragement from men who felt that a woman could do the job. They said it was time for a woman to be in control and to be in a governance position within the union. The union leadership, however, publicly supported and campaigned for a male candidate. My own experiences indicate that the male leadership resists the involvement of females because they feel threatened by us. In contrast, the male membership is much more enlightened and open to endorsing a woman. So, in my victory the first of many barriers was broken. Of course, in this case, it was also the most important.

I hasten to point out that not all men qualify for admission to the "old boys' club." Those who are progressive in their views of women do not fall into this category. As well, there are some women who are welcomed into the club simply because they are pawns of the "old boys" and do nothing for the advancement of women or our cause.

While you can accomplish many things as an activist or volunteer, you have to be in the room where decisions are made in order to have any impact on the decisions. It is important that women are elected to positions where decisions are made. Women bring a different perspective, whether it is at the bargaining table, at a cabinet meeting, or in the corporate boardroom. But our views can only be translated into action if we are in a position to make a difference.

Affirmative action positions play a valid role. There are attempts in some organizations to placate women with affirmative action positions, but we just simply cannot accept that as the beginning and the end of our involvement in politics at any level. Affirmative action positions have to serve as stepping stones for more women to gain access to the full scope of positions within organizations.

It is disconcerting that there is a theory that something is wrong with having the support of women. During my first campaign, a non-supporter expressed his concern that I would get the female vote. He did not suggest that the male candidates might have a similar base of support. The results in both elections indicated that my support was from the overall membership. There was a view by both men and women that it was time to recognize that a woman could do the job and that there was a strong and exceptionally qualified female candidate running.

The fact that women may not run for elected positions is based on a number of reasons. As young girls, historically we have not been encouraged to speak up or take on leadership roles to the same degree as boys. There are also obstacles which many women encounter. Women are usually the primary family care-givers and do not have time or energy to attend union or political meetings or to become actively involved. Secondly, there tends to be fewer role models for women in politics and less exposure to female leaders. Thirdly, it is often more difficult for females to raise the money to finance major political campaigns. Men have connections in the corporate world and through their fraternal and other clubs. Women do not have the same corporate networking abilities because they have not been a part of that environment. Therefore there is less chance for networking to fund political campaigns and to find workers.

You may wonder why we encourage other women to seek political office. The more women who become involved, the more role models there will be for young girls and the easier it will be for women who are currently in positions trying to make a difference. My role as a female union leader will become easier each time another woman gets elected, not only within the labour movement but also at government levels. This benefit applies equally to those who climb their way up the corporate ladder. The exposure of women in top leadership positions will ultimately result in the acceptance of women candidates, increased support for them, and a more equitable sharing of real power structures.

I am not talking about tokenism. I am not talking about a political party running a woman in a seat or position that can not be won or encouraging a woman to run and then providing little, if any support. The biggest single thing we can do as women is to support each other, work for each other, fund each other, and vote for each other. We have to accept this as a fundamental fact of political life. If we are not in the key positions, it is difficult for our opinions to be heard, and for our positions to be put forward. Of course, we must be cognizant of women who are dominated by the "old boys' club" and who will not support progressive women or, if elected, will only serve to toe the line for the "old boys."

It is imperative that women who attain positions of power not forget their roots. It is pointless for women to achieve positions of power and then abandon their sisters in the trenches. The labour movement has made many achievements and accomplished a lot, but we still have far to go. We need women to be in the forefront. We need women who are prepared to take on the challenges. We need women who are bold enough to jump over the daily hurdles that are strategically placed in front of them. And we need women who are willing to persevere, to overcome the barriers. It is not an easy task, but it can be very fulfilling. All it really takes is a sense of adventure, skin as thick as leather, and a determination and commitment to make a difference.

In Sisterhood and Solidarity,

Carol A. Furlong
Secretary-Treasurer of the Newfoundland and Labrador Association of Public and Private Employees (NUPGE/NAPE)

Dear Sister:

It is so important for Sisters of all generations and diverse experiences to join together in our struggle for equality. As a young Sister writing to you, I believe we need to be dedicated to the principles of "Re-Sistahood." So, I offer you the following as a theme to move forward together with and to guide us as we fight to win:

Radical **E**quality = **S**isterhood **I**n **S**olidarity + **T**aking **A**ction + **H**olding **S**trong!

In Sisterhood and Solidarity,

Natasha Goudar
SFL Youth Coordinator

Dear Sister:

As I think back over the years of my involvement in the labour movement, I have some very fond memories and certainly some moments that I wish did not happen. It doesn't seem that long ago that I was in a position you may be in today: learning about unions, about the House of Labour, as well as channelling my energy as a woman and a trade unionist into areas I believed in.

I began working in a nursing home at the age of 16, and by the age of 17 I attended my first union meeting and I was hooked. Hooked, not because I necessarily believed in unions, but by my personal interest in helping people.

By choice, I moved very quickly through the education processes set up within the trade union movement and educated myself on where unions came from, why they were required, and how they worked to assist women. At the same time, I also saw the larger role unions played in the community and the work they did to assist those who were not union members, and this I believed to be just as important.

To say this was difficult for a 17-year-old when my friends from high school were focusing on where the next party was going to be, and who was going to date whom, would be an understatement. It was very hard to relate to other young people when I was spending the weekend at a school learning how to be a shop steward while they were hanging out at the local mall.

This was a choice I made, and one I don't regret, but many a friendship was lost due to their not understanding what I was trying to achieve. At the same time, I truly was trying to find myself, and I sometimes wondered if this was really what I wanted to do. As you know, these are tough decisions to make at any time in life, let alone when you are still a teenager.

Looking back now, I don't regret for one minute the choices that I have made. Yes, at the time I made some personal sacrifices, but in the long run they worked out for the best when I chose to get married, buy our house, and have a child later in my life.

What's it like to work, then and now, in a movement still dominated by and large by men? I believe, as a woman trade unionist now in 2002, that it has made me stronger and more committed to fight the struggles to make the changes we need. As I think back to the earlier days, there were some challenging times. If I spoke forcefully at a convention, I was told I was shrill and strident. If I cried at a meeting over any issue, I wasn't tough enough. If I wasn't able to be available every evening and every weekend, I wasn't committed. If I didn't wish to sleep with a number of male members, I was considered an oddity. If I partied, I was criticized, and if I didn't party, I was criticized.

I survived, as have many other women in this movement, and the fight for equality for women remains my priority. We cannot have real solidarity and unity without equality, and we cannot achieve equality without solidarity among us in society. All in all, I am a stronger woman personally and professionally, and it truly is a movement that I love to be a part of. And I encourage you to join in the struggle.

In Sisterhood and Solidarity,

Heather Grant-Jury
President, Winnipeg Labour Council

Dear Sister:

Women belong in the labour movement. We make it stronger, and all our Sisters benefit directly with better wages and benefits.

Thousands of women in Ontario, collectively, earned millions of dollars more because of pay equity legislation. That law came about through the efforts of Sisters across Ontario who worked together and successfully lobbied for it. And we had fun while we did the work. And we celebrated the fact that women got better wages because of it. And then we kept working for more women to be covered by the law—and won that, too.

These types of struggles and victories that Sisters "in the next generation" take on, and win, will help us all.

Enjoy these times, and always remember to take time to stop and smell the roses and celebrate Sisters in the movement.

In Sisterhood and Solidarity,

Irene Harris
Executive Vice-President, Ontario Federation of Labour

Dear Sister:

I know this is presumptuous of me, but I believe it is my responsibility to make things easier for those who follow behind me. I would like to share a couple of principles with you that I have learned over the years through experience, in the hope that they are useful principles for you in the shaping of your future.

I've been involved in women's issues for most of my adult life. Sometimes I feel like we've made great progress. I see the attitudes of young women, including my daughters, assuming gender equality is a right. Equal pay for work of equal value is an issue like that. Many young women I have spoken to believe in equal pay for equal work, and further that the value of the kind of work they do is as important to the success of that work as someone else's is, and that it is ridiculous to take an opposing opinion.

This assumption is both frightening and gratifying. It is gratifying because, as a young woman, I always dreamed of a world where economic justice for women was not controversial and was an accepted value. It is frightening, though, because there seems to be little attention paid to the fact that we have not yet achieved economic equality. Court battles still are being waged to receive wages which are owed under the pay equity legislation. Unions are working hard to ensure women receive what is due to them, but the process is slow and costly, and in many ways these payments come after years of economic struggle for women that was unnecessary. Additionally, women's wages still trail men's level of income by about 30%.

Principle #1:

So progress is being made. Wonderful. But there is always more to do. We need to be tenacious to keep up the long-term battle and also be positive to be able to see and celebrate progress so we don't get disheartened and stop fighting for what is right.

Other times I see the signals of continuing battles I thought were won long ago. The right to reproductive choice is one of those issues. Sure, in the U.S. *Roe vs. Wade* was a landmark decision in 1973 that gave women access to reproductive health services that were previously illegal, dangerous and underground. In Canada, abortion was legalized under some specific conditions. The battle has been focused around where and when services should be available. It has been long and ugly, but the law allowing for abortion services remained in place although the services were not always easily accessible.

Recent events in the U.S. for providing pregnant women with increased social security to account for the needs of their unborn child, however, threaten the fundamental legality of reproductive health services, which include abortion. The premise for *Roe vs. Wade* is being challenged and the precedent set by the decision may be overturned if legislators proceed with their plans to provide social services to a foetus, since they will be saying that a foetus is indeed a person. This would be the first round in the attack on reproductive choice for women. This may mean a long and difficult time for women and their right to control what happens to their bodies, and the rest of their lives may be jeopardized again. Out of this example I find two separate lessons.

Principle #2:

Our rights, which we may take for granted today, can be taken away with a stroke of the pen. If we are not engaged and vigilant at all times, we will not even notice legislative changes which limit our freedom of choice on this and many other basic issues.

Principle #3:

Not all attacks are frontal assaults. We have long been accused of having "eyes in the back of our heads." I believe they are there so that we can cover our backsides. Why else would we have this uncanny ability as women, except to protect ourselves, and those we love, from more subtle strategies designed to weaken us?

I want to finish up with an anecdote which I think demonstrates one of the most powerful principles I've experienced. In the early 1980s, the Manitoba Federation of Labour (MFL) found itself embroiled in a debate about the role of the Equal Rights and Opportunities Committee (EROC) of the central labour body. The EROC had taken a position to join the Coalition for Reproductive Choice in the province of Manitoba. As noted above, the battles around service delivery were where much of the debate on reproductive choice took place. Correctly, I believe, the MFL Executive Council took the position that the EROC was a standing committee of the federation, which took its direction from convention and from the Executive Council between conventions. The MFL had no policy on the issue of reproductive choice at that point in time, and therefore the Executive gave EROC direction to remove itself from membership in the Coalition.

The MFL Executive Council could have had a debate and made a determination on what the MFL position on choice would be until convention either changed or ratified their position. The MFL Executive Council chose to take the position that labour should stay silent on this issue. What followed at the next MFL convention was predictable. The EROC put forth resolutions to have the issue of reproductive choice debated and policy developed. But this anecdote is not really about the issue of choice. It is about the fact that many women in the labour movement believed that the MFL Executive Council would not have taken a decision for "no position" if there had been women represented on the Executive Council of the MFL.

The affirmative action movement was at work in our communities and there were rumblings among labour women that it was time to have representation of women entrenched in the MFL constitution to ensure that the elected positions were representative of all of the membership.

Another woman and I met the MFL President for lunch one day to make him a proposal to have two positions on the MFL Executive Council filled by women. We indicated that, since their decision on choice, it was believed that the MFL Executive Council was not representative of the feelings of women in the labour movement, and EROC had discussed this at their meetings. We indicated that there had been subsequent meetings with many women who were not officially part of the EROC, as well. We told him there were 40 women at the last meeting in my basement that was called on short notice, and they were members from a broad selection of unions. We said we wanted the Executive Council to put forth a resolution to convention to change the constitution to require at least two Executive Council positions be established for women and elected at the upcoming convention. If the Executive Council were not prepared to push this change, we would target two of the men currently on Executive Council and run candidates against them. They would have to wait and see which two we would choose.

The President left that lunch having agreed to take our proposal to Executive Council and support it. The Executive Council made the decision to set aside two seats on Executive Council for women and asked us to indicate who would be running for those positions. We went through EROC to canvass for the names of women who would be interested and able to sit on the MFL Executive Council, and sought balance between public sector and private sector women. Two women were subsequently elected to the next Executive Council, and the rest, shall we say, is "herstory."

The fact of the matter is that there had never been large numbers of women attending strategy meetings in anyone's basement, but we used the political climate in the labour movement at the time to push our agenda for equality even further. We eventually told the President this about 20 years after that important change in direction took place. The focal point for educating our brothers in the labour movement was at the leadership level from then on, which allowed for greater and faster change in our own structures and policies. This spilled over into better quality, more inclusive positions being taken in society generally, since often the labour movement is the catalyst for the changes occurring in the workplace and being discussed in public debate.

Principle #4:

You have as much power as they think you do. Use it to help everyone share the power and soon the difference you see can be amazing.

Sister, as you can see from my writing, we have not achieved our goal yet. If there is anything valuable in what I have told you, please use it in your struggle for your equality. It's yours. Progress may be slow, but it can be constant. Recognize it. Celebrate it. That good feeling is what keeps us striving for more.

In Sisterhood and Solidarity,

Susan Hart-Kulbaba
Staff Representative, NUPGE/MGEU,
Former Director, Labour Affairs, Crocus Investment Fund,
Former President, MFL

Dear Sister:

So, there is a storm about us. At times it feels as if all we can do is wait it out. The windows rattle. We want to stay inside, find comfort with our loved ones. We light candles.

But then the roar grows louder and we realize that the storm is not a terrifying act of nature. We catch glimpses of distant battles fought on mucky and dangerous terrain. Sometimes they fade into the mists before we realize what has happened, and then they move thundering around us, gathering us up and together. All of a sudden, the enemy slips away and we are left staring at each other, bloodied and sweating and in tears. It is only afterwards, in the firelight, that we can piece together our stories of the times we are in.

Canadians do not want their social security net to be torn apart. Governments give money back to wealthy taxpayers and say they have to fire thousands of public sector workers, leaving citizens without services because they have no money. Union reps negotiate plant closure agreements with great frustration. Tens of thousands of people are discarded in the resource industries, and the cod fishery closed. Deregulation and mergers toss thousands of others out of work. Governments suspend collective bargaining and impose back-to-work legislation when we go on strike.

In Mexico, plant closures reach record levels, teachers raise massive protests against state cutbacks, a worker is shot by armed thugs hired by his own union, and people walk hundreds of kilometres to demand that fraudulent state elections be overturned by a president who has a rather limited view of what democracy looks like. Unemployment levels soar. Multinational companies come and buy up the nation's public resources. One by one, all of the tenets of the Revolution are set aside in favour of a new "liberalism" that has entrenched the old inequalities.

If each of us stands alone, just outside of the firelight where the stories are being told, history will feel like something moving about us without our acquiescence or consent. Our roles will seem to shadow the principal actors who are remaking our world. Yet somewhere beneath the surface, we know this can't be true. We are not simple observers in this moment of crisis and restructuring. We have breath in us. We have life in us. And the truth is that we are not alone.

Union action leads to increased funding for N.B. nursing homes
The Lord government has announced a $13 million increase in funding to New Brunswick nursing homes, intended to cover increased wages and new positions.

"There is no question in my mind that this additional funding is a direct result of our members having gone to the wall on the issue of workload," CUPE Representative Gordon Black said, referring to the province-wide strike of nursing home workers last summer. (4/4/2002)

St. John's water to remain public
"International water companies have been knocking on every municipality's door to try to get control of water services," says CUPE Newfoundland President Wayne Lucas. "We met with the mayor to assure ourselves that this council wasn't about to give up control of the harbour clean-up." (3/26/2002)

First contract boosts wages for child care workers
22 CUPE members who work as educators at Seven Oaks day care centre in Winnipeg have approved a first contract that gives them wage increases of between 9% and 12.5%. (3/26/2002)

Great win for women hospital workers in Ottawa
The settlement, which has a potential payout of more than $4 million, was reached at the beginning of March when the employer, the now merged Ottawa Hospital, stopped fighting a pay equity compliance order obtained by CUPE. "It's a good validation of the power that women have if they want to pursue an issue", says Donna Panke, former union chair on the pay equity maintenance committee, "and a reminder that the union is only as strong as the active participants in it." (3/18/2002)

Speak in your own voice
Closeness to family, sisterhood, language, culture and caring for others were also among the comments from about 30 Aboriginal CUPE and HEU members from across B.C.'s northwest region. The members were in Terrace for a three-day workshop on how to use their union's democratic tools to address Aboriginal issues. (3/12/2002)

B.C. workers say "Liberals are Wrong! Keep Public Services Strong!"
A special education assistant, a library worker, a water treatment worker, a family counsellor, and a young lifeguard helped launch CUPE's Strong Communities fightback campaign in Vancouver this week. (2/4/2002)

Secondary picketing legal
The Supreme Court of Canada has handed down a landmark ruling confirming that secondary picketing is legal. Defined as "picketing in support of a union which occurs at a location other than the employer's premises," the Court agreed with the Retail, Wholesale and Department Store Union.... In its ruling, the Supreme Court says, "Labour speech...is fundamental not only to the identity and self-worth of individual workers and the strength of their collective effort, but also to the functioning of a democratic society." (1/28/2002)

Call for support: Queen's students protest deregulation of fees
Students at Queen's University are currently occupying the office of Principal William Leggett, in an effort to prevent the deregulation of fees for the undergraduate Arts and Science program.

Each of us must find our circle of fire, our places for reflection, our sacred time spent with our sisters. Today I'm sitting alone at my desk in front of a sunny window, so I went to the CUPE web site to listen to my sisters tell their tales of victory of the past few weeks (www.cupe.ca). Last night I sat with my sisters as we listened to music and celebrated a long week of struggles that touched each of us in different ways.

And so we do light candles as the windows rattle. We light candles and we sit together in the firelight so that we remember how the battle was won, how we organized together, how we strategized and theorized and telephoned and knocked on doors and handed out leaflets and sat through meetings and in front of computer screens and negotiated into the night and marched down the centre of the street and circled in front of the employer's gate and did our research and got our message out and tried to do it so that everyone of our sisters had the chance to speak.

And we sit and we challenge one another and are confronted with how we didn't listen to our younger sisters and relied on our white privilege or felt the pain of yet one more exclusion, or let our brothers speak for us, or didn't take care of ourselves in ways that will make us stronger for the long journey ahead of us.

In this hyper-liberal age we live in, the white, rational, individual, male, profit-maximizing taxpayer is glorified above all other citizens. Those of us not in that category know very well that we can't do it alone. We can't live without one another. Everything we do is built upon the work of other people.

Over the past few months, this knowledge has settled deep inside of me, while I have been dealing with breast cancer. I have long-term disability benefits only because of the struggles of CUPE members. A few times a week, I go to a publicly-funded hospital for my appointments because of the struggles of trade unionists to keep it public. The female oncologists and nurses and technicians and clerical staff who take care of me are there because of a publicly-funded education system won by women who demanded access and equality.

But there are cracks showing. The Victorian Order of Nurses who come to my house have had their hours dramatically reduced. Sometimes I wait 4-5 hours to see my doctor. My drugs cost thousands of dollars. What do people do without drug plans? And privatization is just there on the horizon.

When I'm not on leave, I work as a researcher and a writer. I used to think I would never know enough to be able to make a difference. Now I think that it's not "how much" we know, but "how" we know that matters. We learn and write and create together, not alone, and our knowing is part of our collective action. If we really know deep-down that history does not automatically get better, that we are part of shaping history, that we do not act alone, that we need to take time to reflect on our actions, then that makes a huge difference!

Our struggles are constant and we need to work together to strengthen our political practices within Canada and across borders. How we do that is not wholly determined by our past, but I desperately need to learn from women who have been at this so much longer than I have. I want to sit with you, my younger sister, and I want to hear you speak of your struggles and your victories. I want to ask you what gives you hope and courage. Most of all, I want us to tell our stories in the firelight, with gales of laughter, for many years to come.

In Sisterhood and Solidarity,

Teresa Healy
Canadian Union of Public Employees

Dear Sister:

These are challenging times for young women and other working people in Canada today.

It is a time of uncertainty. People are concerned about their future. All levels of government are cutting back on the services that provide help to people who need them most. Corporations are slashing jobs and employee benefit programs. The number of secure, good-paying jobs is declining.

And yet, despite all the bad news, we have to remember how fortunate we are to live in Canada and to be thankful for the hard-won gains that women working in Canada enjoy today. We need to remember that most of these gains are the result of the struggles of women and unions over the last century and more.

My own union, UFCW Canada, has roots going back well into the 1800s, but officially became the United Food and Commercial Workers union in 1979. From the very beginning it made a strong commitment to equality, justice, equity, and the protection of human rights. The object of the UFCW Canada, as stated in our constitution, is to "organize, unite, and assist persons, without regard to race, creed, color, sex, religion, or national origin." This also means that we endeavour, at all times, to eliminate discrimination on the basis of age, disability, or sexual orientation.

Also in 1979, UFCW Canada created the Canadian Commercial Workers Industry Pension Plan (CCWIPP). Today, the majority of UFCW Canada members belong to this specialized plan created to provide members with good retirement incomes. It is the largest multi-employer, jointly-trusteed pension plan in Canada, and is an important addition to government benefits providing retired workers with a more comfortable standard of living. It is especially important to retired women, whose average incomes are substantially lower than those of retired men.

In 1981, UFCW Canada once again led the way when Local 1977 in Cambridge, Ontario negotiated a cents-per-hour training contribution as part of the collective agreement with Zehrs supermarkets. All contributions were deposited into a jointly-trusteed education fund. Initially, the money was used for union education; later the program was expanded to include job-specific training such as meat-cutting, bakery, deli, produce, grocery, and seafood management.

Because of the phenomenal success of this training initiative, UFCW Canada established a National Training Program (NTP) in 1990, to facilitate the establishment of training centres all across Canada. As of 2002, with the help of the NTP, eight UFCW Canada locals had succeeded in establishing dedicated training centres, and several other locals are offering a substantial number of courses at the local's offices or in rented facilities. Training is especially important for women members who are laid-off or seeking improved skills to find better jobs and higher incomes. For women, training is very important for ensuring equity on the job.

UFCW Canada also offers a number of scholarships to members and their children for post-secondary study. Many UFCW Canada locals also have their own scholarship programs.

In 1988, the Executive Board of the UFCW Canadian Council approved the establishment of a fund to provide financial assistance to UFCW Canada members who are political candidates in a provincial or federal election. The fund was established to facilitate political activities, to encourage members to become candidates, and to support the political parties which most closely represent the interests of working people. Federal and provincial legislation determine the quality of life for women and their families, both on-the-job and in the community. It is important to have women in government to represent our issues. As a result of UFCW Canada's program, we now have one UFCW Canada woman member—Bev Desjarlais—in Parliament, and another—Deb Higgins—is the Minister of Labour in Saskatchewan. Another former UFCW Canada member—Carolyn Jones—is also a provincial government member.

In 1989, UFCW Canada established a Women's Advisory Committee. It consists of local union representatives who are active in women's issues. The committee meets several times a year and is responsible for developing policies specific to women's issues, conducting women's conferences, and assisting both the national office and local unions with issues of concern to women.

These issues include pay equity, employment equity, and family benefits: issues which are of particular importance to women workers. Of course, women also enjoy the other benefits that the union negotiates for all workers, such as safer workplaces, improved wages and working conditions, and paid dental and other health benefits.

On the issue of pay equity, UFCW Canada women members were some of the first, several decades ago, to have equal-pay-for-women clauses negotiated as part of their collective agreement. These women were assured they would receive the same pay as men doing the same job. More recently, pay equity has been redefined to mean equal pay for work of equal value. This is an important concept, because jobs that are predominantly filled by women often pay less than those staffed mainly by men, even when the women's jobs require a greater amount of education and skill.

For instance, women who worked in the federal civil service, in jobs such as librarians, were traditionally paid less than men working as custodians. As a result of the work done by unions, who pressured the federal government and took them to court, these women eventually (after 15 years) achieved pay equity, including a retroactive settlement.

Although pay equity has been legislated in certain sectors, in some provinces there are still many women workers who do not have equity. UFCW Canada works with other unions and equity groups to lobby governments to ensure that all women workers can achieve pay equity.

Working women in Canada who don't belong to a union earn on average less than 80% of what a man earns. Women who belong to a union earn about 90% of that earned by male colleagues. Even when there is pay equity in a workplace, women need employment equity to ensure the promotion opportunities that will enable them to have the same wages and benefits as men do. As long as women are assigned to lower-paying jobs and lack promotion opportunities, they will not be able to earn the same as men, even if they have pay equity. That is why it is important to legislate employment equity, which requires companies to create opportunities for groups which have been historically under-represented in more senior jobs. These groups include women, members of visible minority groups, Aboriginal peoples, and people with disabilities. UFCW Canada is working to ensure employment equity for all these groups, including women.

Family benefits are another very high priority for most working women. Unions were instrumental in establishing paid maternity leave and also in lobbying the federal government to extend paternity benefits in 2001. UFCW Canada continues to work with provincial governments and employers to ensure that these extended benefits are made available to the individual workers who require them. Many UFCW Canada locals have also negotiated clauses, as part of the collective agreement, that provide other family benefits. These can include extra paid days off or extended leaves of absence to care for ailing family members. At least one UFCW Canada local has negotiated a partial return-to-work option for new mothers. This allows return to work on a part-time basis so that the new mother, and her new baby, have more time to adjust to her return to work.

UFCW Canada is also active across the country in lobbying for better child-care options for working families. Our goal is an affordable, high-quality, universal child-care which would be available to all who require it. Because of the work unions have done, the government of Québec now provides quality child-care, at a cost of only $5 per day.

Violence is another issue that is especially of concern to women, as many women are the victims of domestic violence or violence in the workplace. Every year the UFCW Canada Women's Advisory Committee spearheads a campaign, as part of the annual White Ribbon Campaign, to raise both money and awareness to combat this problem. UFCW Canada has brochures, posters, and other forms of educational materials to help reduce violence against women. It also works, through training programs, health and safety committees, and clauses in the collective agreements to reduce the incidence of violence in the workplace. For instance, workers who are concerned about working alone at night have negotiated a clause in their collective agreement which requires the employer to have a minimum of two people on duty at all times.

Sexual harassment is another issue that particularly concerns women. UFCW Canada has many educational initiatives, including workshops, to eliminate harassment. Any member who is harassed need not suffer in silence. She can get assistance by speaking with her union steward or contacting the coordinator for women's issues at the UFCW Canada national office.

UFCW Canada's primary concern is with the welfare of its members, but it also appreciates the importance of ensuring good pay, benefits, and working conditions for all workers. That is why our union is constantly reaching out, thought informational pickets and other means, to unorganized workers in retail stores like Wal-Mart and in other sectors of the economy. As long as there is a huge gap between the wages of unionized workers and workers who don't belong to unions, employers will demand that unionized workers take pay cuts so that these employers can more easily compete with non-union employers. So the best way to maintain good pay and benefits for unionized workers is to organize more non-union workers.

The UFCW Canada Women's Advisory Committee also works to eliminate child labour, in Canada and around the world. As women, we appreciate the importance of having children in school, rather than in the workforce. Therefore we work with other unions and activist groups to stop child labour through legislation and public awareness. Child labour is an extremely complex issue and ultimately can only be eliminated by providing a living wage for parents so they can afford to keep their children in school.

As you can probably see, I am very proud of what we in UFCW Canada and the whole of the Canadian labour movement have achieved for the benefit of working women in Canada today. I hope your generation will appreciate our struggles—just as we appreciate those of the women who have gone before us—and continue to work to improve working conditions for all women.

In Sisterhood and Solidarity,

Louisette Hinton
UFCW Canada National Coordinator for Women's Issues

Dear Sister:

I know there are lots of people who really want to 'make a difference' in their time here on Earth. It's not just a phrase or a wish, but actually something they really want to do. It never ceases to amaze me that it was my union that allowed me to actually 'make a difference' in my lifetime.

A grade 12 graduate from a small town in South-western Ontario. A student streamed in high school not by my abilities, but my family's working class background. Streamed into a four-year technical program that denied me access to university. A program that graduated blue and pink collar workers. Workers who were supposed to be loyal and thankful to the boss; not trained nor paid to question or resist.

I became a pink collar worker in 1969 by virtue of my father's 'factory job' and my mother's labour as a child care worker. I worked in non-union jobs as a cashier, file clerk and secretary. I was paid poorly, harassed regularly, and never 'read my rights'. Then, in 1973, I landed a job as a data entry clerk at Canada's Crown-owned airline and my life changed, forever. Not because I was now an airline worker, but because I was a *unionized worker.*

My salary increased dramatically, the harassment stopped, and I was given a collective agreement: a book containing 'my rights.'

I was also encouraged to attend union meetings and to take union-sponsored education programs. At the time I was in my early 20s and my free time was spent 'socializing,' so I declined the offers of my union for several years. Since my experience at school had not been entirely pleasant, I also wasn't interested in the education being offered by my union.

Then I had a fight with a supervisor and, instead of getting fired, which I expected, I got rescued by a union representative. In exchange for the 'rescue,' I offered to attend some meetings (blackmail is a harsh word, but would accurately describe how I got involved).

What struck me most once I started to attend union functions was the composition of my union executive. The membership makeup was 73% women, and the executive board and bargaining committee were 100% men. That was in 1976.

Today the leadership in my local is 50% women (still room for improvement), and my union activity spans more than 25 years. How time flies when you're having fun! How time flies when you're actively engaged in building a better world!

I've held numerous positions in my union and have been the 'first' woman to be elected to a number of them. I've hit the glass ceiling; cried myself to sleep at night; felt guilty about time missed with my children; argued with corporations, governments and union colleagues; and not once—not for one single solitary moment—have I ever regretted the decision to get involved.

There are few guarantees in life, but I can offer one that's fool-proof: get involved with your union and move from simply having a job to your job being your way of life. *Guaranteed* you won't ever regret the decision!

In Sisterhood and Solidarity,

Cheryl Kryzaniwsky
Director – Education Department, CAW-Canada

Dear Sister:

About 350 delegates, overwhelmingly men, were packed into a ballroom at the Royal York Hotel in Toronto. I was sitting in the front row, off to one side, my eyes alternating between the row of guys at the head table on the stage and the men speaking at the floor mikes.

This was no ordinary meeting. It was the December, 1984 Council of the United Auto Workers. The debate was the stuff of history. Led by then Canadian UAW Director Bob White, the Council was deciding whether or not to leave the UAW international union and form a new Canadian union.

The Canadian and U.S. sections of the union had diverged on the crucial issue of contract concessions demanded by corporations during the depths of the recession early in the 1980s. The UAW tried to sell the notion of concessions as necessary to keep the companies afloat. White's classic retort was: 'Workers don't need a union to walk backwards.'

Local leadership from auto, auto parts, aerospace and elsewhere took the mikes in response to White's report about the UAW's position of trying to sell concessions to the membership and refusing to give the Canadians autonomy to chart a different path. They argued that workers have to resist, to fight, to defend their past gains. Corporations would take advantage to roll back the clock. It was unspoken, but you felt that they knew the potential costs of such a fight. And so their courage, their eloquence, their loyalty was all the more poignant. Wow, this was the place to be. These were workers who believed in fighting for progress.

It was my first UAW Council. My union, the Canadian Air Line Employees' Association, was a group of about 7,000 airline workers, mostly passenger agents, about 70% women. Anticipating the impending turmoil of the privatization of Air Canada and the deregulation of the entire airline industry, we were on the brink of merging with the UAW. Over the last few years, we had rapidly gone from being a rather well-behaved employee association, where some were shy about calling themselves workers, to being a scrappy, feisty little union. This was partly in reaction to the polarization of the times, and, I like to think, partly because of a new generation of more militant activists.

What would happen when our two organizations came together? One mostly southern Ontario, mostly manufacturing, mostly men. The other made up of national bargaining units, mostly transportation customer service jobs, mostly women. This meeting was the beginning of the merging of our cultures, and the beginning of huge changes, not only for our airline group, but for the auto workers' total union. From where I was sitting, the straight talking, gutsy speeches were a refreshing change. I felt right at home.

Our group of airline workers did merge with the UAW-Canada, which later became the Canadian Auto Workers union. We were the first of more than 20 unions that would later merge with the newly independent CAW.

In early 1986, several months after the merger, I was appointed by Bob White to the UAW/CAW national staff. As one of only a handful of staff women in a sea of men, I was entering a pretty macho environment. I was a new mother, still nursing, coming back from maternity leave with my youngest son. Although anxious about finding myself in a hostile environment, I was also determined to succeed. My husband took an unpaid leave from work for six months to care for our son while I got started in my new job.

For the first few years I was on staff I was thrilled, exhausted, and learned so much. I was asked to organize the first CAW human rights conference in 1986. It was an emotion-filled and sometimes angry event, yet so gratifying, because we were on the move, fighting to address the serious concerns that members were raising about racism and harassment.

The CAW had also launched a major campaign against the Mulroney government's proposal for free trade with the United States. We held leadership meetings, put out terrific materials, engaged in public debates. The country went from apathy to polarization on the issue.

As the mother of young children with a job that demanded long hours and for which I often needed to travel, guilt was my constant companion. There were tears and some self-doubt, but what job could be more satisfying? It was a struggle to create the space for my family; without the support of my husband Carl our family could not have taken the stress.

In 1990, then National President Bob White appointed me as his assistant, responsible for women's programs, succeeding Carol Phillips who had gone to work for the Bob Rae NDP Government. The CAW had a strong record on women's programs and human rights and I felt so honoured, and a little intimidated, to be given the responsibility of carrying these programs forward. Pioneers in our union like the Local 222 women's committee in Oshawa that pushed to get the human rights law changed to include sex discrimination, former national staff rep Edith Johnston, former organizing director Lorna Moses, an Aboriginal woman in a key national post, Roxy Baker, the first woman elected to the National Executive Board, UAW organizer Sophie Reuther, and so many others were the bedrock on which were built the rights that all women enjoyed.

In 1991, I was asked to organize the first national women's conference on the topic of violence against women. The CAW Council women's committee, led by the chair, Dianne Hollingshead, played a key role in planning the conference. We collaborated closely with the broader women's movement.

The conference was a cathartic experience. Women spoke about their experiences: everything from workplace harassment to stalking to physical violence. It was overwhelming. What was clear was that the union needed to make ending violence against women a real priority.

Then-CAW Council President Frank McAnally had attended some of the conference plenary sessions to hear the guest speakers. He was very moved and agreed to help us take a tough resolution on violence against women to the CAW National Executive Board and to push it to our constitutional convention later that year. The debate at the convention was big and emotional, with both men and women speaking out about their experiences with gender violence. The resolution passed unanimously, as did a policy paper on affirmative action.

This latter paper gave us the union go-ahead to create new residential leadership courses for women and people of colour. These courses were aimed at reaching out to groups in our union who weren't adequately represented, helping them identify barriers, and strategies for building greater participation. They were union building courses that greatly strengthened the participation of these groups. Separate organizing like this was necessary to build participation in the overall union.

We knew that women needed a strong base of support from other women to avoid isolation and burn-out. By the early 1990s, this base of women activists was growing in the CAW, especially as more women got hired in the traditional manufacturing sector, but also as we merged with new groups of workers, many of whom were women.

As this base grew, so did our ambition to make equality gains in collective bargaining. The huge advantage that women in unions have is that they don't have to rely on governments to make change: they can get issues dealt with at the bargaining table. By 1993, the year when we were about the go into negotiations with the Big Three auto companies (GM, Ford and Chrysler), women had an agenda for change to take to the companies.

To succeed we needed to get the key leadership on side. With few exceptions, they were men. But the top national officers, Buzz Hargrove and Jim O'Neil, gave us strong support. The union stood for progress on human rights and women's equality. They created a lot of space for us to push our agenda forward. This was not without debate, but we always knew that we had support in principle.

The 1993 negotiations with Chrysler Canada as the target would be the real test. Larry Bauer, then chair of the Chrysler master bargaining committee, grilled me on some of our demands. For example, why should the company pay for child-care? Parents have kids, so they should look after them.

He was testing me, looking for arguments to support the proposal, but I didn't realize it then. I reacted emotionally, describing my personal experience as a single parent, working shifts, having to leave my son with a neighbour, never sure how he was being cared for. How desperately I fought to finally get him in a licenced non-profit centre. What a relief. The centre and staff were wonderful. How great it would be if all parents could have this kind of security and quality care for their kids at a price they could afford.

That was good enough for him. We tripled Chrysler's contribution to child-care in 1993 from 1.5 cents to 4.5 cents paid into a fund for each straight-time hour worked. We had already built one child-care centre in Windsor. This money would help us build a second one in Oshawa. But we also had other issues on our agenda.

CAW women were determined to take our concerns about violence against women to the bargaining table. I explained our proposal to the company. If a woman were in an abusive situation at work or at home, for which she had proof, and it was affecting her performance or attendance at work, she would not be disciplined. The company debated: why just women? Why not men? Surely the company would do this, anyway. Why did we have to spell it out in the contract?

Because in over 90% of the cases it's women, not men, who are facing violence or harassment. Because women need to see the heading "Violence Against Women" in their collective agreement so they know that they have the right not to be disciplined, and that the union will back them up. If the company will do it anyway, they should have no problem putting it in the agreement.

We won this language on violence. In addition, we won a pioneering program of "women's advocates" in the workplace. These advocates are specially-trained by the CAW in issues of violence, family law, harassment, and counselling. Women members access them in the workplace on a confidential basis, to be a sounding board for advice, and for referrals to the appropriate services they need. Posters went up in the women's washroom describing the advocates and giving their confidential phone numbers.

To gain company support for the program, we bargained that the CAW advocates and their women company counterparts would all take the CAW-developed training program and annual updates. Their enthusiasm for the program has been an important endorsement.

To fight workplace harassment, we bargained a new joint policy and procedure that is printed in the collective agreement. It includes the key provision that workers can refuse to continue to work if their complaint is of a very serious nature that needs immediate attention.

In addition, we negotiated that there would be a full-time CAW coordinator, paid by the company, to oversee employment equity and human rights for the union, working with the CAW workplace equity reps. These full-time coordinators have played a key role in advancing all equity issues, including the employment equity plan, leadership training on harassment and equity, and in overseeing the handling of day-to-day harassment complaints by the workplace equity reps.

Just as the 1991 CAW convention put in several key equity provisions in the structures of the CAW, the 1993 auto negotiations cemented many key equity provisions into our collective agreements. They pioneered changes that now are being bargained in many other sections of our union. This progress helped our union take a giant step forward in defending our members' rights, both in and out of the workplace.

Today the CAW maintains its core culture based on the auto industry. It's a proudly working class, in-your-face kind of organization with a strong sense of social responsibility. About 30% of our members now are women, and this percentage grows each year. The diversity of our membership is increasingly reflected in our leadership and staff as new faces come on the scene.

Human rights work continues to be a priority, with conferences for human rights, Aboriginal and workers of colour, and lesbian, gay, bisexual and transgender members. And women in CAW have come a long way. There are women presidents of some large local unions. Several of our department directors are women, including the aerospace department. Human rights and equity concerns are woven throughout our educational and program materials. And our National Executive Board recently issued a statement renewing its commitment to work to ending violence against women. At our education centre in Port Elgin, we also recently erected a beautiful bronze statue and an eternal flame dedicated to the women killed in the Montreal massacre. Our new Women's Director, Julie White, is full of ideas and enthusiasm for the future.

As for me, I continue to feel inspired, to work with the growing number of women activists in our union. More of my time has been spent in other areas over the last few years: in political activism, and in bargaining in the airline and hospitality sectors of the union, and most recently in the auto sector, responsible for the Ford chain from the president's office. Whew! Never thought I'd see this day.

Our strategy as women was always to build the union. We organized as women, but allied with men so that we made progress together. The whole union felt good about making change. That's not to say that it wasn't, or isn't, an ongoing struggle.

Equality is always a work in progress. Women today still face many hurdles and so many challenges:

- How do we increase our representation in workplace leadership, especially workplace bargaining committees?
- How do we make women's structures and programs, as well as those throughout the union, as inclusive as possible to attract the broadest range of women activists?
- How can we generate new enthusiasm for pay and employment equity and make them a reality in all workplaces?
- As the union continues to evolve, bringing in new members in new sectors, how do we maintain the core CAW identity in this new evolved form?
- With a changing economy and growing numbers of low-paid, marginal jobs, how do we reach out and organize those who need a union most?

- As more women slip fall into poverty in our increasingly polarized society, how do we finally turn the tide and win with a new political vision for Canada's future?
- And how do we finally, *finally*, gain quality, universal child-care for kids in Canada?

Our common goal in the union is to advance workers' rights in a society that is increasingly hostile to workers' interests. New young women activists in the union today still have their plates full.

In Sisterhood and Solidarity,

Peggy Nash
Executive Assistant to the President, CAW-Canada

Dear Sister:

Greetings from Port Elgin.

I'm up here for the CLC Ontario Region Winter School for three weeks. Much as it is crazy at times, it is also the best of times. How often do we get a group of 150 trade union activists and leaders in an educational setting for a whole week? It is where links are forged and solidarity strengthened. I just wish that we could bring more youth so that they could feel the energy and the optimism.

There is a new statue installed by the CAW to commemorate the victims of the Montreal Massacre. It is a statue of a young woman student in jeans, jacket, and a knapsack around her back. She is standing and looking over at the Eternal Flame on the far side of the pond. Right by the woman statue, there is a plaque engraved with the following :

"We pledge we will work to transform our world so that neither your dreams, nor your lives, are cut short by violence..."

I am struck by her gaze: it is one of sadness, gentleness, longing and hope...that some day soon...

Let me take a moment to reflect and draw the parallel. As trade union sisters, we are also working to transform our labour movement so that neither your dreams, nore your aspirations and voices, will be cut short by violence. In that regard, the violence is not physical, but the violence of silence.

The act of silencing is an act of violence. When a young woman union activist is feeling so intimidated in a room full of experienced and seasoned male leaders that she cannot speak, that is an act of silencing. When an immigrant worker is being told by management not to speak in Spanish to her co-worker—"we speak English here!"—that is an act of silencing. When a woman worker of colour is being told that the union is not ready for her to run for a leadership position, that is an act of silencing. The experience of being silenced can be a scar for life.

As witnesses to the above scenarios and many other similar situations, if we stand by and do not speak out, we are reinforcing the circle of silence. Implicitly, we are accepting things as they are and treating them as normal, without realizing that we are bearing witness to an act of exclusion and denial.

Sister, as someone who started in the labour movement 33 years ago, I am here because of the voices and strength of many sisters before me. For you as a young, new activist, yes, there will be challenging moments, there will be acts of silencing, but please do not be discouraged, do not be intimidated, and, above all, do not walk away from this movement of ours. It is a family that is worth fighting for.

Speak up, speak out, and speak now. In your search for your voice and your place in the extended labour family, we will be there and we will not be silenced.

In Sisterhood and Solidarity,

Winnie Ng
CLC Regional Director, Ontario Region

Dear Sister:

I could have blamed it on the hormones, but I didn't. Probably because those pregnancy hormones were long gone out of my system and I had been—at least if you listen to my husband—abusing that excuse for a good 15 months.

Hormones aside, I just couldn't help myself. After all, patience has never been one of my strong points.

I admit it. I lost it. It being the above-mentioned patience.

My husband and I had taken our daughter, Kate, for her six-month vaccination. While we were waiting in the lobby of our neighbourhood public health centre, trying not to think about our daughter being jabbed with a needle, two women nearby were chatting about the improvements to parental benefits under the Employment Insurance system.

One woman was commenting on how great it was of the government to *give* us a year's leave, and how grateful she was. The other woman agreed, saying she wished she had a year off when her child was born.

I could feel a flush climb up my neck and settle on my cheeks. Before I could think about it, I jumped to my feet, interrupting their conversation with an abrupt: "The government didn't *give* us anything. It's not the government that deserves our gratitude." Two mildly surprised faces looked at me as if I had forgotten to take my medication that day.

But I continued. After all, it was no sense wasting a head-full of steam.

I explained to a less than comfortable audience just who we should be really thanking. The 35 weeks of parental leave—25 weeks more than prior to December 2000—was the result of a long struggle by mostly women labour and social activists. It was no gift. And the job is far from done.

I then went on to ask them what's so great about 55-cent dollars at a time when a family's living expenses have just increased tremendously. This fact alone may make it impossible for many women or men to take advantage of the leave. [Note: Those new moms who earn above $39,000 a year (the maximum amount the government allows us to pay premiums on) take home less than 55-cent dollars since the maximum benefit is 55% of $750 a week or $39,000 annually.]

In fact, I continued, it's not costing the government one red penny since the benefits are paid out of the Unmployment Insurance Account, which is funded by premiums paid by workers and employers.

By now, the two women were eyeing the doorway which I had partially blocked, wondering, no doubt, how they could make a quick getaway. They need not have worried. Just as I was about to launch into another diatribe about the federal government's dependency on the UI surplus, the public health nurse came looking for Kate and to their rescue.

The experience did get me thinking about how little is known about the tremendous strides made for women by other women, especially by women and their unions.

It's not so long ago that working pregnant women had to quit their jobs or take vacation when their babies were due.

There was no such thing as paid maternity or pregnancy leave until 1971, and at that time women were only entitled to six weeks after the birth of their child, although they could take eight weeks off before the child's birth.

Women would wait 12 more years before any improvements were made to maternity benefits under the Unemployment Insurance system. That's when the benefit period was made more flexible and adoption benefits were introduced.

By 1989, after a major court case found the UI Act was discriminatory because natural parents were not entitled to parental benefits, the Act was changed to include 10 weeks of parental benefits. That meant women were entitled to 15 weeks of paid pregnancy benefits and 10 weeks of parental benefits which could be shared between the mom and dad.

It wasn't until 2000 that the additional parental benefits were introduced, resulting in the year-long leave. The first 15 weeks (plus a two-week unpaid waiting period) are for the mother, while the 35 weeks of parental benefits can be shared.

Women trade union activists know that many quality-of-life gains have their roots in the labour movement. An explosion of women's participation in the labour force and an increase in the number of women in unions have resulted in countless advances in the area of equality over the past 30 years.

Women's ability to negotiate collectively have resulted in a long list of bargaining victories, such as pay equity, employment equity, maternity leave top-up, flex-time, job sharing, compressed work weeks, reduced work time, paid personal holidays, family leave, and contract language around violence against women.

But union women have not been satisfied to reap for themselves the benefits of their bargaining work. We have fought and continue to fight for equality for non-union women. That fight has carried us into the streets and into the political arena as we try to convince the political elite of the need for social and economic equality.

One such example is the CLC's ongoing UI campaign, headed by Sister Nancy Riche. She has been determined to keep this issue atop the CLC's list of priorities. The campaign has been in large part responsible for creating awareness about the country's unemployment insurance system. It has educated people about the cuts to the program and detailed what an unemployment insurance system that meets the needs of today's labour force should be. And, through this work, many positive changes have been made to the program since the cuts of 1996.

It is a fact that women in unions enjoy greater benefits and a better standard of living than non-unionized women. For example, many unions have negotiated maternity and parental leave top-up as well as extended leave. These steps and others are critical to women's economic and social equality.

The International Labour Organization (ILO) sets the minimum standard for maternity and parental benefits at 66% of a worker's average wage. In Canada, the benefit rate is 55%, compared to

100% in France, Denmark, Norway, Switzerland, the Netherlands, Austria and Germany, and 80% in Iceland and Finland.

The ILO has said that the progress in maternity leave protection over the last 50 years has "failed to resolve the fundamental problem experienced by most, if not all, working women at some point in their professional lives: unequal treatment in employment due to our reproductive role."

Women in the labour movement have learned that it is critical that we take an active part in negotiations to ensure that our issues and concerns are included in the bargaining agenda.

I believe it is important that we celebrate our victories. But most of all, we must recognize and thank the women who came before us. They have made what we have today—and will have in the future—possible. They have laid the foundation on which social and economic equality will one day become reality.

My union sisters, as you fight for equality and a more just society, I sincerely hope you pay tribute and celebrate the amazing accomplishments of the women who have come before us. I have many women to thank for blazing the path that has made our world a better place. One of those women is Sister Nancy Riche, whose immense contribution to the Canadian labour movement is distinguished by her analysis, commitment, leadership, common sense, humanity, and legendary sense of humour.

But she's also a friend, who has encouraged, led and inspired women from coast to coast to coast. I'm one of those women. I am honoured to call her friend and grateful that my daughter will also have an opportunity to know and be inspired by her.

Thank you, Sister!

In Sisterhood and Solidarity,

Lana Payne
FFAW/CAW, St. John's, Newfoundland

Dear Sister:

If what you're looking to read is a version of 'we've come a long way, baby,' this isn't where you're going to find that story today.

Yes, when I started out as a young trade union activist in the Canada of the late 1970s, it was a sexist, agist, racist, classist, patriarchal society. And, although a lot has changed, so much has stayed the same or become worse for women and girls today.

We daringly called ourselves feminists and challenged the male elite wherever we found them. And I know it's passé now to talk about feminism, in the same way I grated at the term 'women's lib,' but whatever you chose to name yourself, my younger sister, the same challenges are all still there.

I've had a few "firsts" in my life, but, although they seemed important at the time, the power structure never shifted. I was the first elected woman union chairperson of my bargaining unit at Bombardier Aerospace, the first woman negotiator for the Canadian Auto Workers, and the first woman assistant to the President of our very militant and male union.

There were so many other gutsy trade union women around making their own individual breakthroughs that it felt for a moment in herstory like we might shake the foundations of the male hierarchy that ruled us for so long. That we might not only be taking up positions of influence, but that we might use that influence to change the structures of power itself.

Those were the days of 'affirmative action' when we could unblushingly talk about the setting of quotas to ensure space for women and workers of colour and people with disabilities in non-traditional areas of work. When we pushed the glass ceilings that held women down and hammered on the doors of the "boys' clubs" that locked us out. Those were the heady days of 'pay equity' when we were unashamedly forcing the recognition that 'women's work' was undervalued and compensation was overdue.

We fought for freedom of choice and the right of women to have abortions. We demanded the right to control our own bodies.

We were convinced that the obvious logic of universal child-care meant we were well on our way to winning the first new national social program since Medicare. For a brief shimmering moment, the idea of ever-increasing equality and social justice found a momentum that seemed unstoppable.

There were warnings, though, that the gains we dreamed of were vulnerable.

In 1989, I had the privilege of working on the campaign of Audrey McLaughlin, who was to become the first woman leader of a national political party in Canada. It was a tough, dirty fight, with the male candidates making deals with each other for support in order to try to stop our campaign. We had a woman leader who talked about such different and threatening ideas as the democratic process and group decision-making. When we won, after an all-out battle headed by a majority women's team, it was exhilarating and inspiring. It felt as if we had the world by the tail and now anything was possible, any boundaries could be pushed.

And then, with breathtaking suddenness, they pushed back!

In December of 1989, women engineering students at the Ecole Polytechnique in Montreal were separated from the male students and 14 were shot because they were women in a male field and because their murderer considered them 'feminists'. I know you've learned of this piece of herstory in your schools over the years, but for so many of us it was an end to innocence that we've never quite recovered from. It was a first signal of many to come that you can't just fit women into the existing system: the system itself was inherently unjust and had to be replaced.

And in the ensuing years, affirmative action became employment equity and then was maligned as 'reverse discrimination' and undone with enthusiasm by right-wing politicians. Yet our brothers in the union didn't rally to the defence of the cause, either, saying that maybe we'd gone too far too fast.

We've seen public programs eroded, public education threatened, and national child-care not even on the agenda. Once again, a woman's right to a safe abortion is under threat.

It seems that we may have mistaken the rattling of our chains for the shaking of the foundations—because the male elite is still as strong as ever.

And now we live in a world where there is more wealth than ever before, and yet more women and our children die from lack of basic necessities of life than ever before. Where billions continue to be spent by men on the toys of war, and yet clean water and basic medicine is denied to millions of human beings. In a world where corporate profit takes priority over the standard of living of the majority of the world's people. And where a fundamentalism that enslaves women around the globe also denies us an equal role in decision-making.

So, my sister, if you don't want to, you don't need to take on any label. You don't need to call yourself a feminist or radical cheer-leader, or anti-capitalist. But you must know that the battle has only just begun, and you need to decide if you are willing to fight alongside us.

In Sisterhood and Solidarity,

Carol Phillips
Director, International Department, CAW-Canada

Dear Sister:

When Nancy Riche first told me she was putting a book together, I was delighted. Nancy has reached out to sisters in the labour movement throughout the international community, and she and they have many wonderful stories to share—inspiring stories of our sisters' progress in the ongoing struggle for equality.

I should have known Nancy's book would be a collective effort!

When I first met Nancy, she was Education Director at NUPGE/NAPE and Eastern Vice-President of the Newfoundland and Labrador Federation of Labour. It was early in the 1980s and I was the secretary and a shop steward with NAPE Local 3102 in central Newfoundland. At the same time, I was starting to become an activist. I was also meekly trying to assert myself as a feminist. Nancy Riche was instrumental in motivating me to continue on the path I was travelling, and she has been a wonderful mentor along the way, even when she has been thoroughly pissed off with me.

From Nancy I learned the importance of listening when other sisters speak. The solidarity and spirituality that develops from sharing experiences, celebrating accomplishments, and supporting each other in the continuous struggle for equality and social justice helps heal many wounds.

I learned that being a trade unionist was synonymous with being a feminist, and, if you were both of those, the odds were good that you were also a social democrat.

I learned that enjoying the benefits of inclusion doesn't mean you are prepared to ignore the ugliness of exclusion.

I learned that, while it was tough being a woman in the labour movement, it was a whole lot tougher if you *didn't* have a union to represent you.

I learned that an injustice to one, in any part of the international community, was an injustice to all, and if we want things to change, we have to challenge and change them collectively.

But, most important of all, I learned how to stand up for my principles and be strategic about doing it—even if means appearing unreasonable at times.

I will never forget the genuine expression of both pleasure and pride on Nancy's face when I walked into my first CLC Executive Council meeting as the Vice-President for Newfoundland and Labrador. I knew she was gleefully adding another name to her tally as she did a visual sweep of the sisters sitting around the table.

Nancy, you have been a friend, a mentor, and a true sister to trade union activists in this country and around the world. As one of the many sisters who have been blessed with the opportunity to know you, I thank you for your conviction, your courage, and your contribution to the greater good of humankind. You have instilled such great hope in all of us; there is no question the struggle will continue.

Our younger sisters who are just starting to take their places in the labour movement will grow from their own experiences, but they will also learn from yours.

Nancy, in addition to being a legend in your time, you are a very special human being.

We love you just for being you.

In Sisterhood and Solidarity,

Elaine Price
President, Newfoundland and Labrador Federation of Labour

Dear Sister:

I'm so pleased that you are now standing here beside me. I know it's not an easy decision to be here, but believe me when I say the rewards are great.

No other movement gives you the forum to take on the challenge of protecting and enhancing local, provincial, national, and international women's, human, and workers' rights. Nowhere else will you have the opportunity to work side by side with so many other dedicated women who will celebrate your successes and be proud for you, and share your sorrows as if they were their own. And I believe in no other segment of society will you have the support of so many union brothers who believe as we do that women's achievements create a better society.

But to be honest, I'm sorry to say that not all of our sisters and brothers will support you, and many may try to get in the way of your accomplishments. It's not an easy ride, dear Sister. Some will tell you that there is first time to be served, that you don't have the experience or expertise to carry out the tasks at hand, or that you simply don't understand enough of our history to carry the torch.

Some may tell you "it can't be done." Well, let me tell you that finding solutions is what we do best. We are the mediators, the problem solvers, the healers, and the compassionate listeners. We crave knowledge and continually strive to learn new things.

Don't let anyone else's limitations become your own.

Stay balanced in your life. Make time for family, friends, and most importantly, yourself. Let your heart guide you through every situation, while listening only to the positive thoughts in your head.

Know that there will be dangers and pitfalls, and even a misplaced step.

But I promise you this: If you remain honest and true to the principles that have brought you here today, you will have my support and assistance when you need it. My hand will be extended whenever you reach for it. The energy that passes between us will give us both renewed strength.

No one is giving you your place in our movement. You must take it and make it your own.

Thank you for your energy, your commitment, and the compassion you bring to our piece of the world. I look forward to every moment we have to spend together, and hope the fire in your eyes will continue to burn bright. And some may say (including me): keep that fire in the belly, too.

Let me end with a few words that inspire or make us feel good.

Pledge allegiance to yourself
Believe in miracles
Leap before you look
Dive in—and laugh a lot along the way
Live out loud
Dare to make mistakes
Listen to your own wise and gentle voice inside—don't ignore it
Love who you are
Breathe deep, trusting breaths
Follow your dreams—wherever they lead you
And last but not least, demand nothing less than everything.

In Sisterhood and Solidarity,

Angela Schira
Secretary-Treasurer, B.C. Federation of Labour

Dear Sister:

"You're not going away again, are you, Aunt Mary? You're never here! You're always going to meetings and stuff. Don't you ever get tired?"

My 14-year-old niece, Meaghan, stares wide-eyed at my well-worn suitcase and briefcase overflowing with papers, bending down to pick up a stray paper and tuck it back inside. "What do you do that is so important that you have to be gone for my birthday party?"

"It's part of how I do my job as a union representative," I explain as I give her a quick kiss, throw my things in my car, and get ready to leave. "I promise, as soon as I get back we'll go out for dinner, just me and you, and we'll celebrate your birthday all over again."

A huge feeling of desperation totally envelops me, just like the fog that is rolling in from the ocean on this cool May morning, forcing me to slow down on the road. I hope that the sun will soon burst forth and burn off the fog, so I won't be too late for my meeting. I've been asked to address a group of high school students about the role of unions. The last class I spoke to knew very little about unions. In fact, when I asked them what words came to their minds when I said "union", their responses included words like "mob," "violence," "protecting bad workers," etc. It's so frustrating at times, being a union rep. I sometimes feel like I just keep running into a brick wall. So, why *do* I do it? How would I answer my niece's question?

As I drive along, I think about how fitting it is that my niece's birthday is May 1. I make a mental note to make sure I tell her about that historic day when we meet for dinner. In fact, I realize, May Day is probably the reason why I do what I do, and all of a sudden I know exactly how I am going to answer Meaghan's question.

May Day: the International working class holiday. Although it originated in pagan Europe as a festive holy day to celebrate the first spring planting, the real reason it became a worker's holiday evolved from the struggle for the eight-hour day in 1886. On May 1, 1886, national strikes were held in the United States and Canada for the eight-hour day. At the Chicago strike, police killed six strikers. The next day there was a rally in Haymarket Square, and a bomb exploded, resulting in the deaths of many protestors and police. Eight labour leaders were arrested in connection with the bombing, even though there was no evidence against them. They were tried and sentenced to death, mostly because of their beliefs.

May 1 was declared an international working class holiday in Paris in 1889, and became recognized in every country except the United States, Canada, and South Africa. But rather than suppressing labour and the struggle of working men and women to fight for change, the events of 1886 actually mobilized many generations of activists.

Eventually, workers won the eight-hour day, and throughout history many other gains were won. Some of the struggles were not as violent as the Haymarket Square incident, but make no mistake about it: every gain took some kind of struggle to attain.

Arriving at the school, I look down at the eager faces in the assembly hall, young men and women Meaghan's age. I tell them about May Day, and the reason why unions exist. I talk about 1945, and the Ford strike in Windsor, where workers won union security, and where the grievance procedure replaced the right to strike during the life of a collective agreement. The students hear about how unions won many benefits for their members over the years and how women, who have historically been discriminated against, have made huge gains because of unions. I explain to them why we call ourselves "sister" and "brother."

"So how will that help me?" chimes one young woman in the back row. "That was then, what about now? I work at MacDonald's, they don't have a union. I'll probably never be a union member, even after I graduate. I can fight for myself—why do I need a union?"

"Excellent question, dear sister!" I respond. "Workers have the right to join trade unions. We won that right, as well. But the reality is that there are many workers who do not have unions to speak directly for them. Let's look at what the union has brought to them, besides the eight-hour day."

I take out the newly amended copy of the Labour Standards Act. We examine the changes that have just recently been made, based in large part from input by trade unions. Minimum wages, as inadequate as they may seem, at least set a minimum rule for employers. Tips belong to the workers, vacation is a right for everyone, maternity leave and benefits did not always exist but are now enshrined in legislation. Every worker in this country now has the right to work without harassment or other forms of discrimination, and in an environment that is healthy and safe.

I spend the next few hours talking about workers' rights, and the importance of unions both then and especially now. I talk about social activism, and the issues that unions are always involved in, like opposing violence against women, fighting against sweatshop working conditions for children all over the world, and trying to elect politicians who will speak up for workers in Parliament and provincial legislatures. There are lots of questions, and time flies by. Soon, it's time to leave. I know I made a difference in how most of those students view unions now, and I feel very proud to belong to a union.

The sun is beginning to set as I reach the hotel. Another night away from home. I grab a quick bite in the hotel restaurant, and settle down with my book back in my room. Sure, it's a lonely life being on the road, and yes, I am missing an important family event. But that's okay, because what I do is also very important, not just for the union members I represent and the students I speak to. I know that what I do will make life a little bit easier, and a lot more fairer for Meaghan and her children down the road, and deep in my soul I know that's worth more to me, and her, than a piece of birthday cake.

As I get ready to bed down for the night, I feel elated. I can't wait to get back so I can take Meaghan to dinner and tell her everything that I am feeling. And just as I am about to doze off, it dawns on me: she already knows!

In Sisterhood and Solidarity,

Mary Shortall
National Representative, Canadian Labour Congress

Dear Sister:

You belong to a union. You are not alone. You have power.

There are three kinds of power: power *over*, like racism and sexism; power *within*, which is inner strength and self-confidence; and power *with*—solidarity, sisterhood and community, which is Union Power. And you are now part of a movement which links your home, your community, your workplace, and your Union in a vision of a society where everyone is equal and peace and security are the foundations of life and liberty.

The goal of the union movement is to build a respectful workplace environment where workers are empowered and treated equitably and fairly, and with respect and dignity.

It's time for a history lesson. Let's take a short walk through women's history and through union women's history. I want you to realize the rich heritage you have embraced. I want you to be aware of what unions and union women have had to face in the wake of much adversity to get to where we are today, and to provide you with a safe work environment, good pay, good benefits, security, and trade union rights.

Women's work has historically been unpaid, underpaid, undervalued, and is still, in my opinion, "never finished," or, as my mother used to say, "A woman's work is never done."

Did you know that women do two-thirds of all unpaid work in Canada? Equal sharing of housework occurs in only 10% of two-wage-earner households, according to Statistics Canada. Statistics say it all: women do $11 trillion dollars worth of unpaid work globally each year. All over the world women are trapped in job ghettos and in employment relationships offering no benefits and meagre pay.

I knew from an early age that my mother was a brilliant woman. She stayed at home and raised nine children. After all, what were her options? When she graduated from high school and applied to do nursing, she was rejected because she was five feet tall and weighed only 95 pounds, and one of the prerequisites to enter nursing school was that you had to weigh a lot more than that and stand a lot taller,

I guess. I, for one, never forgave the people who made those rules. Are you starting to get the picture?

It wasn't until 1925 that women over 25 years of age in New-foundland were extended the franchise and were allowed to vote in elections, and only a few years before that that women in other provinces of Canada were given the vote, finishing up in the province of Quebec where women were finally allowed to vote in 1940. Not bad, I guess, considering that it was only in 1929 that the British Privy Council deemed women to be "persons." As late as 1947, by law, married women couldn't work for the federal government, and it wasn't until 1955 that these restrictions were lifted. Rich history, indeed!

Dear Sister, there was so much discrimination—you know, treating people differently, negatively or adversely, without a good reason. In Canada, the French, the native peoples, and women all were the targets and the victims of grave injustices. Racism and sexism flourished. It took the Quiet Revolution in Quebec in the 1960s to empower the French-speaking citizens of that province.

The Canadian Labour Congress has defined affirmative action for women as any action designed to remove barriers to equality, overcome past and present discrimination, and improve the economic status of women. The affirmative action debate spilled over into Canada from the United States in the late 1960s, and in 1970 the Report of the Royal Commission on the Status of Women was published. Women and visible minorities saw vast improvements in their lives when the debate was translated into laws and into action. They saw doors of opportunity open up for them for the first time in history. This was a program of positive measures obviously meant to atone for past injustices and to protect against future imbalances in group participation. Those who make arguments against affirmative action are in fact supporting the negative actions and the discriminatory practices of the past.

We have much to be proud of as trade union women. While all these changes were erupting in society, women in unions were working hard to ensure greater measures of protection and benefits for their sisters. Where collective agreements existed, the law now gave the unions the right to negotiate the entrenchment of affirmative action programs into the contracts in order to protect them from unilateral change. Things were changing rapidly for women: we were distancing ourselves from the tokenism eras of the 1960s and 1970s; women were gaining self-esteem, high morale; and the entire social fabric for women was being reshaped.

All of these events had positive impacts on our social, political, cultural, and economic lives. Women were empowered and women were speaking out loud. Women brought forward the real issues—maternity and paternal leave, child care, sexual harassment, employment equity, family responsibilities, health and safety, equal pay for work of equal value, or pay equity—and it was union women who led the fight and who joined with strong like-minded women to change our society forever.

Union women organized. They came together inside their unions and formed Women's Committees made up of women whose purpose was to represent women's issues inside the union movement. And what a job they did! The brothers in the union were forced in a lot of cases to share some of the power, to defer to women on issues where they lacked that expertise. Most unions were sensitive enough to assist women in creating an environment that encouraged and supported women to become more active, both inside and outside of the union.

The objectives and the goals of the Women's Committees were to provide opportunities for women to gain leadership skills, organizational skills and confidence-building skills. Union women were suddenly getting elected to attend conventions, to decide union policy, and to run for union office. Once the women were allowed to have their say, things inside the union and outside the union would never be the same again. And we are all eternally grateful for that.

But you know what? Don't jump up and down yet. We did accomplish a lot and probably we grew weary along the way. Since a decade or two have passed, women now find themselves on the slippery slope once again. Affirmative action seems to be a thought from the past and women are thought to have crossed the threshold and accomplished that equal footing; but hold on, things don't just progress without nurturing. And it is time we started nurturing women's issues and women's lives once again. I believe we have started to slip behind, and I think it is time we as union women took up the gauntlet once again.

Women are care-givers, women work in home care, women work in child-care and elder-care—and this work is still not considered to be of a professional nature that would warrant wages and benefits that would allow these workers a decent standard of living. While there is still one woman, one man, one child, who is underprivileged, our work remains unfinished.

Dear Sister, your work has only just begun. We need you and all our sisters and our brothers to carry on the struggle and to ensure that hard-fought gains are maintained. Our focus must be clear: that women's lives must continue to improve; that women do realize equal pay with men, considering that currently women employed full time in Canada receive on average only 72% of men's earnings; that women are not subjected to sexual violence and harassment; and that women are given all the support systems necessary to ensure that their children are nurtured and cared for and protected. These are but a few of your challenges in the union movement, and since you've been such a good student, I have every confidence that you are up to it. After all, "a woman's work is never done."

In Sisterhood and Solidarity,

Marie St. Aubin
Staff Representative, Canadian Auto Workers (CAW)

Dear Sister:

I am going to begin by telling you a little about myself. My name is Susan Taylor, and I am 25 years of age. I work at the Delta Hotels and Conference Centre. I am from St. John's, Newfoundland, and I have been involved in my union for five years. I never really understood the importance of being involved in my union or any union until a little over a year ago. A union to me means job security and a right to voice my opinion about what I see and what can be done to get more people involved in believing in the Union.

As a casual, I never really was told what my union does for me. I feel that this is a very big factor in why people don't understand why they pay union dues. If you don't know what something is there for, then why should you care if it is there in the first place? The youth within my workplace do not know what a union is, and chances are they don't care.

As shop stewards, it is our duty to treat all employees equally and represent them to the best of our ability. The problem is that the majority of youth who are in my place of work are casuals and don't know the slightest thing about what the union is here for. They barely work, and, as for myself, I am a night auditor so I have trouble getting to them on a regular basis.

Another problem is that the senior staff tend to say negative things about the union. Well, I feel at some point the union affects everyone—whether they see it or not. If they only could realize that, if you don't have job security, then there goes your great pay, your benefits, your vacation, and everything that people have fought to get you all these years.

Years ago I worked in non-union places, and the difference is you work to live and nothing else matters when you make $5.75 an hour. If people could see what their dues are for and what a young woman or man in the labour movement means in this day and age, they would be amazed how far we have come. Without the union we could never get what we deserve in the workplace.

When we talk about the labour movement, I wish that more people knew who Tommy Douglas was and what he contributed to the workforce and labour movement. He helped people to have more rights and a voice that can and will be heard for generations to come. If we don't start getting youth involved now, then who will be left in the labour movement one day? I feel that this could lead to a lot of trouble within unions. We can't just depend on the people who are involved to get their children involved. There are a lot more voices that need to be heard and given the chance.

From becoming involved in different areas of the union, I feel that there is a lot of favoritism that should never be when we talk about union representatives and things like that. If you work in a non-union place, then fine, hire your friend. But a union is a much bigger deal. Now we are talking about something that people have been fighting for forever. It is not about who you know, it is about a person who cares and believes. It would be unjust to give someone a job or position when we all know someone else who will give it so much more of their heart.

Every job I have ever worked at I truly can say I have enjoyed. I am much happier within the union, though. If I had never been hired at this job or learned about how great a union is, then I would just be another voice that would have never been heard. All voices need to be heard. It would be a great accomplishment in the making—especially when people listen.

As a young women in the labour movement, I think we need to be strong to be the individuals we are. I don't think that one person is any different from any other in regards to doing a job. We are all out for the same goals: to live, work and survive. I feel that, when people say that there is a difference in all unions, this makes me very upset. I believe that all of us should work together for one goal—to fight for our rights and have a voice that will be heard. How can one union be better than the next? Are we not all out for the same thing? If we can go to a rally and do it in support of any labour organization, then how is it that people can say they dislike another union? If they are trying to overhaul the system and run things, fine, but I think we all should believe in what's right.

A little while ago, I was chosen for a youth internship for my Local 1252. I went to many places, learning all about the labour movement. I was in Toronto at one point where Dave Kilham, a great teacher of the labour movement, taught ten of us from different locals about privatization, human rights, globalization, and as much about the labour movement that you can absorb in 13 days. Now, this internship was also a great learning experience because we all got to "shadow" a union rep. I shadowed Larry Zima. I sat in on disciplinary hearings and I watched as a man did a job that not all people could do. It was a job that consists of having great knowledge and a lot of caring about what you believe in.

This is how I see the union. You go out believing with your heart, knowing that this person you are defending and fighting for totally deserves your representation. Isn't this what all unions are out to do? Doesn't that make us all equal? I truly feel this is true. We may all have different collective agreements, but we all want what is fair because we all deserve it, and this is what I think Mr. Douglas believed. I would only hope this will stay this way forever.

We now have to get people to go with us and vote left, so we can be heard and have a stronger voice, and all work together for a better work environment and more rights—because we deserve them.

Let's talk about discrimination and harassment. Many different people work in many different places. There are all kinds of jobs in this world. I work in a hotel, and I love it. When a man or woman jokes with me, it makes my job go faster and I have fun because I know they are joking and I am comfortable with them. But every workplace has different people with different personalities. I don't think in all cases harassment is an issue. I feel it is how comfortable you are with the people you work with. If someone I don't know well comes up to me and says something horrible or disgusting, I will put them in their place.

Like I said, though, everyone has different personalities. In Newfoundland, we are known for our hospitality and things like calling people "honey" or "darling." Now, I feel anyone who thinks being called "honey" is sexual harassment is totally off base. If it is said with a sexual context, of course, then you may get offended, but you can usually put such persons in their place. Some people just go way too far with what is and isn't harassment. If you truly feel you are being harassed, then by all means do something about it. But I think that too many people ruin other people's lives over just words when it would be enough just to tell someone to stop. Make sure you always have a witness so you feel more comfortable. I know there are definitely circumstances that are very serious, but I am talking about people who are out to make a few dollars.

Another example is that recently, while attending a conference in Toronto, I purchased an item to help support a union. When we talked, we spoke about human rights. As I went to leave, I said, "Thank you, ladies." One woman called me back and said, "I thought you believed in human rights?" I said, "Excuse me?" She then said, "We are not ladies, we are women." Can you imagine if I had said, "Thanks, women"? It just doesn't sound right to me. I told her that my mother had raised me to always be polite and courteous. I was really upset by this incident. How is it that some woman can tell me I don't believe in human rights because I called her a lady? This is what I mean when I say people take things too far. I will always call a lady a lady. I believe this is a very polite thing to say.

When I did my internship, we were all very upset by some clauses in the Human Rights Act. Now, I know that it is law in a lot of cases, but I still have freedom of speech and personally I love to be called a lady. A woman is who I am, a lady is what I want to be. A law is a law, but I feel that some things just get taken way too far, and for someone to correct me on something that I said that was very polite, well, maybe she has too much time on her hands.

One other thing I would like to talk about is that I sometimes feel that people who have been in the movement for years think that because we are young we know nothing. Well, I did encounter this attitude while at a recent conference. Another person I was with did also. We were both told we should listen and that we didn't know who we were talking to. Now, I did listen, but I am just as important and I should receive the same respect back. The problem I see within the union is that everyone is surposed to agree because they are told to. Well, I disagree because people who disagree with how things work are the ones who go far in a union because they have a voice and aren't afraid to use it. I do not think this happens to everyone, but I feel we are all entitled to our own opinion and to express it.

Unions sometimes kind of remind me of politics, and I guess it is all politics. I find this very sad, but hopefully it isn't all about the money—it is about our rights. I think the union is about stating your ideas and discussing them with your local or a caucus to let people know how you feel. It is good to gather as much information as you can before you speak up, but sometimes the people who don't speak because they're shy or afraid are the ones with the best ideas.

Well, as a young women in today's labour movement, the points I have written were to give ideas and show how I feel. Obviously not all people think the same. I would like to close by saying I believe I am one of the people today who are totally all for the union—and you will not hear a lot of youth say this or feel this way. I believe in the union and I truly feel we can all make a difference. We must educate and do all we can to keep the movement strong. I say this with all the enthusiasm in the world.

In Sisterhood and Solidarity,

Susan Taylor
Shop Stewart, UFCW Local 1252

P.S.—I forgot to make the point that I think that all the collective agreements and the union constitution should be put in plain English.

Dear Sister:

How can I tell you what I have been through as a union woman, what I am going through today, and what we are all destined to go through in the decades ahead? You know, I don't really feel inclined to explain to you just how difficult the road has been because, when all is said and done, all the obstacles along the way were worth it. And there has been more to it than just fighting. We have gathered together, we have laughed, we have shared our solidarity, and we have celebrated our victories.

Talking of victories, it would be remiss of me if I failed to mention what will be recorded as a historic event, one of which you have no doubt heard. I am talking about the settlement of the complaint brought by PSAC members against the federal government regarding pay equity. We had to fight for nearly 16 years, but our perseverance was rewarded and our pay equity complaint was settled. After years of joint studies, court hearings, grievances, demonstrations, occupations and protests of all kinds, we won our case.

Our victory is not confined to a few thousand federal public service employees. The most important pay equity settlement in the world is a victory for all women who demand justice and equality. The courts took their side despite all opposition. At the time of our victory, we received accolades from sisters throughout the world, from as far away as Australia. They wanted to let us know that, together with us, they had been impatiently awaiting the outcome of our solidarity and perseverance.

This same energy guides our efforts when we participate in major events such as the World Women's March, the People's Summit, and the 1+1 Campaign, to name but a few. I have always believed, and I continue to believe, that we can change the world.

Nor am I inclined to give you an account of the history of union women because the real history books will tell you better than I can. Instead, I want to talk to you about what we can achieve together, regardless of the period in time, regardless of the cause in question, and regardless of the magnitude of the challenge. I also want to tell you that, if you commit to this path, you too will know what it is to grow with your sisters and to work to build something great for your children and grandchildren.

These upcoming generations are counting on all of us to protect their environment, to defend their right to public services, to protect their universal health care system, and to ensure their individual and collective security. It is up to us to stick together in a time when these rights are threatened, both by the cowardice of our governments and by the tenacity of multinationals.

When I started participating in union activities, the men were the leaders, those who gave our movement its direction. Later, the feminist movement grew to such a point that it spilled over into our area, in the union environment, because we had to assume our rightful place and because it was time for that to happen. It was time for our approach to be adopted in what were traditionally male environments. And so today there is nothing more natural for you, sister, than to consider being a shop steward, a local chapter president, an alliance facilitator, a picket line captain, a speaker, or national president, without doubting your talents or the place reserved for you in your union. You *are* the union! The union is the co-worker you see every day.

You know, I rather envy you your lot. All the splendid projects for you to pursue! Pay equity, for which I have fought for over 15 years, has been, if not entirely, at least to a large extent, achieved. Where in the past the call was for tolerance in relation to people from visible minorities, the disabled, gays, lesbians, bisexuals, and Aboriginals, the barriers are starting to come down, one by one, so that you can be free of the prejudices that can only impede progress.

You look around, and you will surely say to yourself that we experienced union women are talking about another world that no longer exists. You probably believe that women's equality has been achieved in your own world and that you have the power to do whatever you feel inclined to do. That is why we need to look further afield and make sure that we do not forget our sisters who still face problems with poverty, violence, and discrimination. We must also understand that globalization will have an adverse impact on women's economic security and on our rights as people.

Sister, today the whole world is ours. Unionism goes far beyond your workplace and is spilling over into the social movement. I hope that you lack neither ambition nor courage, for you will be called upon to defend not only union principles, but also social and political principles affecting people you have never seen but to whom you might speak by virtue of modern technology, and whose suffering and reality you know. Fortunately, you have learned that your sisters and brothers do not necessarily look like you or speak your language, and will not always live in your area. The smaller our world becomes, the more important it is to maintain our solidarity.

Like us, you will have major challenges to meet, but I am convinced that you are up to the task. I have confidence in you and in our sisters. Today's union women must prepare the way for the young who want to take action, whether it be in the union, the political arena, or society at large.

What I ask of you today, sister, is that you remember the women who paved the way for you, that you fully live up to your union, social and political commitment in today's world, and that you make sure there are others to take over the task, others who, once again, will not look like you but will want to walk in your footsteps to cross frontiers we have not yet imagined.

In Sisterhood and Solidarity,

Nycole Turmel
National President, Public Service Alliance of Canada

Dear RE-SISTAH,

this letter that I'm writing is not conventional
but intentional
to let you know just what you see
is me

not the token youth, or only youth
but a sister with a role
who
wants solidarity to be an action
not a word
who
tries to ensure that solidarity is with our sisters and brothers
in the Third World

that's me
plainly

while women workers still face bumps
on what many think are paved roads
our lives will be lived in the best of struggles

and until equity equates equality for all
poor, marginalized, and small
young sisters will take a stand
older sisters give us your hand

not just on the street for equal pay
but demand an end to world wide war
for
we are the leaders of today
not the future of tomorrow

thank you to the hands that brought our sisters up
allowing us to demonstrate
and dedicate
our lives
to those like we
re-sistahs
who
see homophobia, racism, ableism, and sexism as the plague
who
hate that classism rules the day

damn all the hands that bring our sisters down
end the oppression
and plan for your succession
don't move aside
but beside

let the leadership flow on down
no frowns
just rise
with smiles that reach your eyes
and know
that we will take the revolution where it needs to go

In Sisterhood and Solidarity,

Monica Urrutia
the first ever CLC Vice-President for youth (PSAC)

Dear Sister:

I often wonder how I came to be who I am: a trade unionist, feminist, and social democrat. I was not attracted by the politics of either movement; and it's certainly not a career path that you can map out and move. In fact, most of the women in leadership in the movement will tell you that it was an accident; they were in the right place at the right time; or just a matter of luck. For me, it was certainly all of the above, plus some anger over how I—and most other women—were being treated by their employer, by their government, and even by their union!

It was 1975, International Women's Year, and I was teaching mostly young women in a community college. What a consciousness- raising year—for me and them! The more we learned, the angrier and more determined we became.

I chose the labour movement and the NDP to raise my voice and concerns. It made sense, and still does—even if it doesn't always meet my expectations.

To quote another trade union leader, "we can't contract out our politics." We must be ever vigilant, demanding and noisy. Not everybody will like you (it would be easier if they did), but you will get things done.

But why do some of us choose to go one way and others another? Some great traumatic event, perhaps—what "they" now call a "defining moment," or a series of events that occur where bit by bit you develop your analysis, strengthen your commitment, and allow your passion to soar, to wear it on your sleeve and come out of your mouth at every opportunity.

I remember a time, many years ago, having dinner with a group of women friends (in fact, it was the Women's Committee of my union, NUPGE/NAPE, in St. John's. One of the women talked about how common it was for families in St. John's to have servants (servant girls, they were called). She said, "My mother had a servant." My immediate response was, "My mother *was* one." I've often wondered why I responded so quickly. Pride? Some sort of arrogance that I had the right to be a trade unionist and she didn't? After all, I was from the right class!

I have never quite figured it out, but I do know that my mother's stories of her life as a maid had a tremendous influence on me, particularly when she insisted that she was not a maid, but a cook.

One story, which she said I could never tell publicly, was about the time she came through the front door of the house in which she was working carrying a bucket of coal. A young boy of about eight was coming down the stairs as she was entering. He told her in no uncertain terms that she was not to use the front door.

She was embarrassed by this story; I was furious!

Her one goal in life, although she never said it, was that all her children would rise above the role of servant. (She probably thought we should do so well that we'd have one of our own!) This goal would be accomplished through education. Her most prized possessions were university graduation pictures; she never forgave me for not going to my own convocation.

She sent us to the "best schools" in St. John's, and she never understood that all the other students came from "the other side of the tracks," and they were not shy about letting me know. I never told her how painful it was for a little girl in Grade 3 to be the only one in the class not to be invited to Maxine's birthday party. I understood very clearly, even then, that there was no invitation because of how I talked and where I lived. (I often wonder if I've embellished this story over the years.)

I never did tell her about the green (form-fitting) coat with "leopard-skin" collar. She had bought it at one of the discount stores for $6. She was so pleased, as was I, with the great bargain. My schoolmates laughed at it! After all, Maxine wore leather and suede in Junior High!

You see, when my mother pushed us to go on to university, to do well, to earn big money, she kept reminding us that we were just as good as anybody; we could be equal to them.

My reaction was somewhat different. My questions were filled with anger and, I guess, humiliation. How dare that little boy talk to my mother that way? Who the hell do they think they are, laughing at my coat—and at that price! (Or, I never wanted to go to her party, anyway.)

Forget the fact that a few friends and I just happened to walk by her house at party time and saw them all in the back yard—but my friends, who didn't go to my school, agreed with me that we wouldn't want to go to her silly old party, anyway.

Others may have deeper, more intellectual reasons for answering this question. I know only that these three events defined for me the kind of society I believed we should have—and can still have. They have helped me to understand that being poor doesn't only mean lacking a lot of money. (They also taught me that having money is better than not having it.)

I could probably not explain class—but I know which one I was assigned to, and even if we had never met, we still would have known something was not quite right.

And now, after all these years of being a trade unionist, a feminist, and a social democrat, I haven't changed my belief of what it is we are struggling for.

Is it too much to ask that we all have the right to go through the front door, and that we all get invited to the (birthday) party?

In Sisterhood and Solidarity,

Nancy Riche
Secretary-Treasurer, Canadian Labour Congress
(and still a trade unionist, feminist, and social democrat)